Praise for *Making Every Science Lesson Count*

Making Every Science Lesson Count is a high-quality book written by an experienced and highly effective science teacher. Drawing on evidence-informed practice, Shaun Allison discusses the principles underpinning great teaching and learning. The principles of challenge, explanation, modelling, deliberate practice, feedback and questioning are carefully and richly illustrated with examples drawn from teaching all three sciences. In doing so, Shaun Allison is making an important contribution to the pedagogy of science education.

This is a book for all science teachers, no matter whether they are very experienced heads of science or science teachers starting out in their careers. It prompts all of us to think about the way we create opportunities for our students to learn about science.

I will use this book to shape CPD with science teachers and it will be on the essential reading list for my PGCE science trainees.

Dr Brian Marsh, Principal Lecturer, University of Brighton

Every science teacher should get hold of a copy of this fantastic book.

Shaun has a brilliant way of synthesising complex research on pedagogy and cognitive science, with each chapter presenting clear ideas with a theoretical underpinning which is bang up to date. His writing is accessible and is brought to life with inspirational anecdotes and stories.

This book would be excellent as a key source of expertise in high-quality CPD – I only wish I'd had a copy when I started out teaching physics.

David Weston, CEO, Teacher Development Trust

Shaun Allison shares the insights of an experienced classroom practitioner who takes tried-and-tested teaching and learning strategies, known to and used by experienced teachers of science, and adds pedagogical significance to them.

The underpinning concept of providing ways to become a great science teacher permeates every page, while the reflective questions at the end of each chapter are a useful way for the reader to encapsulate the key points therein. The foreword and acknowledgements highlight the need to value practitioners whilst promoting the need for, and value of, creativity in science teaching and learning. The passion for science held by the author is evident – such passion is a way to guide learners towards becoming effective and independent students.

Making Every Science Lesson Count will be useful for trainee teachers preparing for PGCE assignments as it requires deep reading to appreciate the plethora of valuable guidance and advice shared. Any teacher undertaking a science subject knowledge development programme will most definitely benefit from the book's pedagogical guidance to supplement their course, while experienced teachers working on postgraduate theses will also find this work of value and will appreciate the teacher-led ideas.

Dr Lyn Haynes, Senior Lecturer, Canterbury Christ Church University, Programme Director, INSPIRE STEM PGCE

Making every science lesson count

Six principles to support great science teaching

Shaun Allison

Crown House Publishing Limited
www.crownhouse.co.uk

First published by

Crown House Publishing Limited
Crown Buildings, Bancyfelin, Carmarthen, Wales, SA33 5ND, UK
www.crownhouse.co.uk

and

Crown House Publishing Company LLC
PO Box 2223, Williston, VT 05495, USA
www.crownhousepublishing.com

First published 2017.

British Library Cataloguing-in-Publication Data

A catalogue entry for this book is available from the British Library.

Print ISBN 978-178583182-9
Mobi ISBN 978-178583253-6
ePub ISBN 978-178583254-3
ePDF ISBN 978-178583255-0

LCCN 2017941649

Printed and bound in the UK by

Gomer Press, Llandysul, Ceredigion

Foreword

I would like to extend my warmest congratulations to Shaun Allison and Andy Tharby on the success of their first book *Making Every Lesson Count*. This detailed work must have taken many hours of thought, research and planning.

When Shaun contacted me, outlining his intention to write another work, my first thought was how does he manage to find the time! I feel honoured indeed to write the foreword for this new publication and expect it to be another hit.

I have spent a lifetime trying to teach science (more specifically, chemistry) successfully. Obviously the pupils must enjoy the lessons and they must understand all aspects of them, so we need to make every lesson count.

When I first started my teaching career in Porthcawl Secondary Modern School in 1967, I was quite shocked! The science teaching involved very little practical work; it was mainly 'chalk and talk'. There were no laboratory assistants or technicians so everything, including washing up, was done by the teacher (usually after school). How did I manage? I resolved to write new schemes of work to incorporate practical skills, request more apparatus and money and spend more time in the laboratory after school.

When I was given the post in Porthcawl, I knew that the school would be made a comprehensive in 1971, and that I would then be allowed some input into the design and stocking of the laboratories. There would be technicians and assistants in all laboratories. Wonderful, I couldn't wait!

One of the biggest problems for teachers across the school was discipline and gaining the respect of the pupils. In 1971, the school also appointed Roger Burnell to set up a drama department. We became great friends, but it was his teaching of the subject that really impressed me. Pupils of all ability were captivated, enthralled and excited by this very talented man. He allowed them freedom to express their opinions, and to suggest ways of improving work themselves but, most importantly, he taught them to have respect for other people and their opinions. Roger taught them how to set up pictures in their minds of how the topic or the character could be portrayed. I was determined to use these ideas in my science teaching.

My main idea was to present science as a series of stories which were all linked together. Of course, the pupils may not understand some of the scientific words, so these would need to be explained using mini stories as well. The language used by teachers must vary depending upon the ability of the classes and the volume of the oral delivery must vary constantly as well, in order to capture and maintain the interest of the pupils.

I firmly believe that drama must play a big part in captivating pupils in their science learning. The budding teacher must imagine the laboratory as a stage and the pupils as the audience. After all, we are trying to get pupils interested in our subject. The more interesting and alive the teacher is, the greater chance they have of building good relationships with pupils. Once this is established, pupils will be enthused and want to learn more about the wonders of science.

Once we have the pupils engaged, we must try to present the material in a logical sequence. I used to plan my lessons for the following week on a Friday night and write detailed sequences of lessons for all classes. I was very fortunate to have excellent support from my technicians and would write a list of apparatus, chemicals and so on needed for the experiments and projects. This same format was used throughout my teaching career.

For me, the most important part of successful teaching is gaining the respect of pupils. Once that is established, and with the help of a good logical teaching scheme, pupils will become engaged and will enjoy the lessons (well, most of them!). Discipline, of course, is essential and should be insisted upon, especially in the laboratory environment.

The good science teacher is the one who loves and knows their subject well and wants to do their best to pass that passion and knowledge on to their young charges. Make it interesting, make it exciting! There is a whole new world out there!

E. E. Clarke, Former Head of Chemistry,
Porthcawl Comprehensive School

Acknowledgements

This book is dedicated to all the amazing science teachers and lab technicians across the world, especially the fantastic science teams that I have been fortunate enough to work with over more than two decades of science teaching. A very special mention must go to the current science team at Durrington High School, of which I am immensely proud to be a part. Our young people couldn't ask for a more committed and hard-working group of scientists to help nurture and grow their scientific curiosity and understanding.

It is these science teachers, working away in schools all over the world, who do an amazing job of inspiring and educating our next generation of scientists. You are the people who create that spark in students, as somebody once did for us, which could lead them down the path of a career in science. It is that spark which creates the doctors, surgeons, engineers and research scientists of the future – and for that, the whole of society owes you a huge debt. You really do create the future.

I would also like to thank the teachers, leaders, researchers and educational writers that I engage with through Twitter and blogging. You have challenged my thinking and broadened my horizons beyond all measure – more than you will ever know – and for that I am truly grateful.

Above all, though, I would like to thank my beautiful wife, Lianne, and my four gorgeous children, May, Finn, Eve and Jude, for putting up with me and making me smile every day. You are my world and I love you all very much.

Contents

Introduction

Science teachers have a huge responsibility – we shape the future of society by developing the thinking and understanding of the next generation of scientists. Science is a vast body of ever-growing knowledge and skills which can prove daunting to students and new science teachers alike. Great science teachers have helped to develop that knowledge through their passion for and commitment to the subject. It is this that helps them to enthuse their students. Over the years, I have been fortunate enough to work with and learn from a number of great science teachers – science teachers who are passionate about their subject and know how to impart the joy of science to their students.

One such teacher was Pam McCulloch, a science teacher at Durrington High School. She started working at the school in 1978, and she taught there until her retirement from full-time teaching in 2014. Over this thirty-six year period, Pam's students consistently achieved fantastic outcomes and many of them went on to brilliant and successful careers within the field of science. Very few teachers achieve this level of excellence over such a long and distinguished career. Pam was an excellent teacher and has very clear views about why science teaching matters. In May 2016 she told me:

To me, science is the most important subject. All other subjects pale in its wake. As science teachers, it is our responsibility to enthuse the pupils so that each generation pushes the boundaries of scientific discovery further and further. This is essential for the continuing advancement of humankind. Without science, we would still be in the caves.

A good science education provides students with the knowledge they need to think deeply about the medical, technological, environmental and industrial problems that will need to be solved over the next century. It builds on our inquisitive nature about the world in which we live and makes us question things, and by questioning we solve problems and advance our own understanding of the world. Even for those students who do not go on to pursue a career in science, it is essential that they have an understanding of how science impacts on their lives. How else can they make informed decisions in an increasingly technological world? Science is the perpetual search for understanding and explanation, and this starts in school science lessons.

In *Making Every Lesson Count*, Andy Tharby and I describe six pedagogical principles that lay at the foundations of great teaching.[1] The first principle, *challenge*, is the driving force of teaching. Only by giving our students work that makes them struggle, and by having the highest possible expectations of their capacity to learn, will we be able to move them beyond what they already know and can do. Challenge informs teacher *explanation*, which is the skill of conveying new concepts and ideas. The trick is to make abstract, complex ideas clear and concrete in students' minds. It is deceptively hard to do well. The next principle is *modelling*. This involves 'walking' students through problems and procedures so that we can demonstrate the steps and thought processes they will soon apply themselves. Without *practice* student learning will be patchy and insecure. They need to do it, and they need to do it many times, as they move towards independence. It goes without saying

---

1 Shaun Allison and Andy Tharby, *Making Every Lesson Count: Six Principles to Support Great Teaching and Learning* (Carmarthen: Crown House Publishing, 2015).

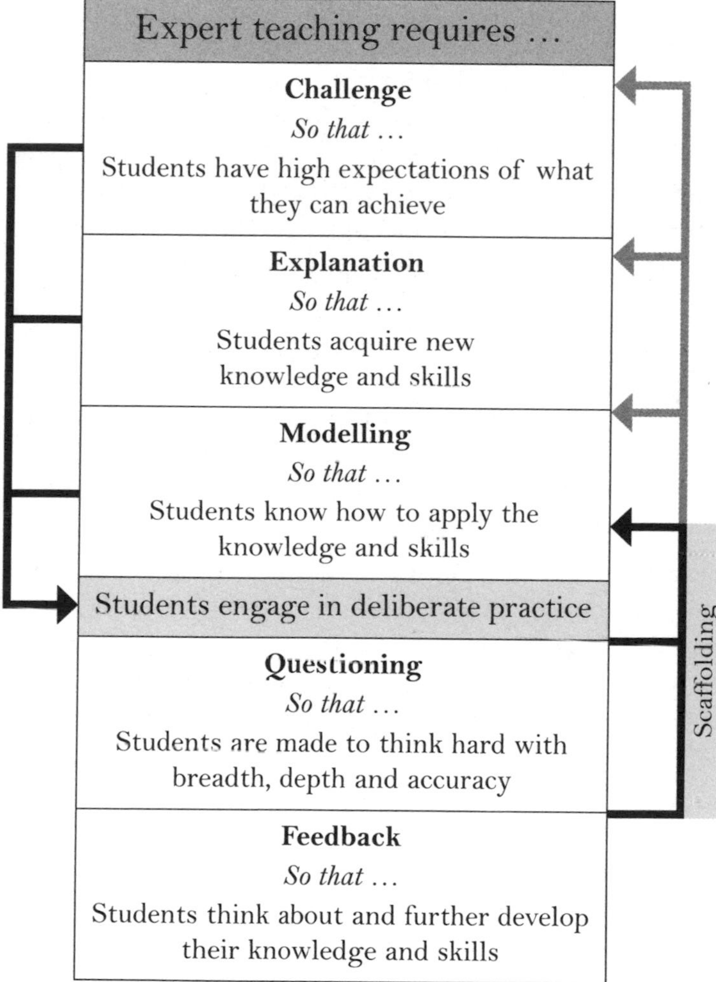
Expert teaching requires ...
Challenge
So that ...
Students have high expectations of what they can achieve
Explanation
So that ...
Students acquire new knowledge and skills
Modelling
So that ...
Students know how to apply the knowledge and skills
Students engage in deliberate practice
Questioning
So that ...
Students are made to think hard with breadth, depth and accuracy
Feedback
So that ...
Students think about and further develop their knowledge and skills
Scaffolding

that practice is the fulcrum around which the other five strategies turn. This is because it develops something that is fundamental to learning – memory. Students need to know where they are going and how they are going to get there. Without *feedback*, practice becomes little more than task completion. We give students feedback to guide them on the right path, and we receive feedback from students to modify our future practice. And so the cycle continues. The last principle is *questioning*. Like explanation, questioning is a master art. It has a range of purposes: it allows us to keep students on track by testing for misconceptions and it promotes deeper thought about subject content.

Great science teaching is aligned with all of these principles; however, they are not a lesson plan or a tick-list. This book will present them as individual entities, but in reality they are members of one body. They sustain each other. Not only do they help you to plan science lessons and schemes of work, but they also help you to respond with spontaneity to the ever-changing and ever-complex needs of your students within lessons.

In recent years, the education establishment has lionised the individual lesson. Indeed, teachers have been enculturated to talk about teaching in terms of how successful or unsuccessful a single lesson has been. The issue of the single lesson, and in particular the ubiquitous three part lesson, probably came about as a result of the following:

- The National Strategies. From 1997 to 2011 the Department for Education produced training materials that were delivered to schools, with a significant focus on the three part lesson.[2]
- The history of Ofsted and schools grading lessons. Although this is now no longer the practice of Ofsted and, thankfully, many schools.

---

2 Department for Education, *The National Strategies 1997–2011* (2011). Available at: https://www.gov.uk/government/publications/the-national-strategies-1997-to-2011.

- The publication of national curriculum schemes of work and their adherence to the three part lesson idea.[3] The legacy of this is still seen within a number of commercially published science schemes of work.

The problem with this focus on the individual lesson is that learning science is not speedy, linear or logical. It is slow, erratic and messy, and it doesn't fit into neat three part chunks. Fortunately, though, there is something that we can use to our advantage. When we explain new scientific ideas, students have a great deal of prior knowledge to build upon. For example, children know that if they hold something in the air and drop it, then it will fall towards the ground. They understand the fundamental principle of gravity. We can exploit this, and then build upon it through our teaching. There are a whole host of real life examples that we can use to supplement our explanations.

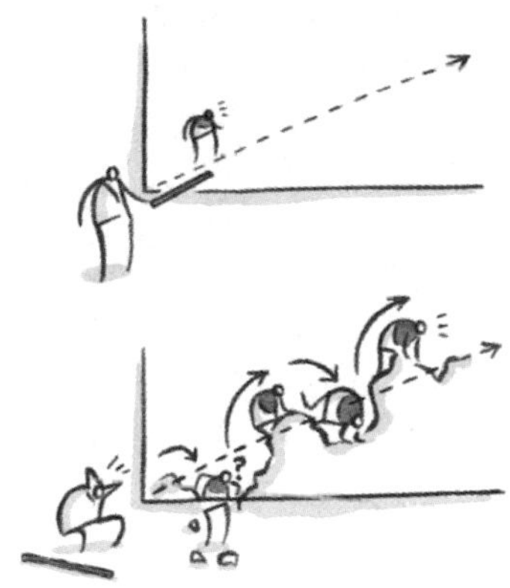

Cognitive science tells us about the importance of storytelling when it comes to supporting good explanations, which is why great science teachers are great storytellers![4] We don't just tell them about the theory of evolution, we tell

3 See http://webarchive.nationalarchives.gov.uk/content/20100612050234/http://www.standards.dfes.gov.uk/schemes3/subjects/?view=get.

4 See Daniel T. Willingham, *Why Don't Students Like School? A Cognitive Scientist Answers Questions About How the Mind Works and What It Means for the Classroom* (San Francisco, CA: Jossey-Bass, 2010), p. 66.

them about Darwin's journey around the Galapagos Islands on the *Beagle* and how he started to observe the different beaks of the finches and how this made him consider how these changes came about by the process of natural selection. We hook them in with a story and then hang the theory around it.

Then, of course, there is the practical work and demonstrations that we do. Again, they lend themselves brilliantly to supporting great explanations, but they are also an essential part of the modelling work we do, which is how we make abstract ideas concrete. For example, once a student has been shown potassium permanganate crystals dissolving and producing a purple streak which, when heated, moves around water in a convection current, understanding the idea of convection becomes so much easier. It also makes it more memorable.

Real life examples can also be used to support the idea of making the abstract more concrete. For example, the theoretical explanation of plate tectonics is quite a challenging concept to understand. However, by linking it to videos and images of erupting volcanoes, earthquakes and tsunamis, we can help students to understand these abstract concepts. This also exploits our inquisitive nature as humans. By showing students videos and images of natural processes they instinctively want to find out what causes them.

John Hattie proposes that there is a difference between surface and deep learning.[5] Simply speaking, surface learning refers to knowing the key facts about a topic, whereas deep learning refers to how we are able to relate, link and extend this knowledge. It's clear to see how this idea is crucial to the teaching of science. For example, once students understand the particle nature of solids, liquids and gases (surface learning), they can use this to explain processes such as melting, evaporation, condensation and convection (deep learning).

---

5 John Hattie, The Science of Learning. Keynote speech presented at Osiris World-Class Schools Convention. London, 2014.

The most skilled science teachers are able to judge perfectly how much time to spend on the surface learning before challenging the class to move on to the deep learning. They understand that there is no point in introducing the deep learning if students are not secure with the surface learning, which also supports effective questioning and feedback.

The six principles are already inherent in the best science teaching. Unfortunately, however, there are a number of challenges for science teachers to overcome. It's worth exploring these one at a time.

High level of content

The science curriculum is packed with content that teachers have to get through at an alarming rate. We know that in order to learn something, a student needs to focus on repetition and retrieval practice (i.e. retrieving items of knowledge from memory over and over again). As science teachers have to move quickly from one topic to the next, to the next, there is very little opportunity to return to key ideas to embed them. It takes lots of practice time to embed key knowledge and skills – a luxury that science teachers simply don't have.

Abstract ideas

Science teachers have to explain a number of abstract ideas that their students can't perceive with their senses. For example, an atom is a very theoretical concept. If students are going to understand what it is and all of the ideas beyond it, such as chemical bonding and the particle nature of matter, then they have to begin by developing their own concrete understanding of a very abstract idea. This makes explanation very tricky.

The tipping point between surface and deep learning

The structuring of learning in science is difficult. We have already discussed the idea of surface and deep learning. While this potentially presents a nice framework around which to build scientific understanding, it can often have the opposite effect. Science teachers will often move on to the deep learning without really embedding the surface learning, which will inevitably result in misunderstanding, confusion and frustration. For example, particle theory is a threshold concept in science – that is, a key piece of knowledge that must be understood in order to make sense of more complex scientific ideas. It is not uncommon for students to have a basic knowledge of the facts (surface learning) but still not be able to get through the threshold because they bring with them naive interpretations and misconceptions based on cognitive misapprehensions of both a conceptual and perceptual nature. For example, many students have a basic understanding of the particle arrangement in solids, liquids and gases, but still have major misconceptions, such as believing that there are gaps between the particles in a liquid. As a result, they may be able to answer superficial questions correctly, while possessing a very limited understanding of particle theory.

Science teachers need to employ effective ways of finding out if the surface knowledge is embedded before they move on. The most skilled teachers support students in developing deep learning by:

- Using diagnostic questioning.
- Addressing non-relevant ideas in a very explicit way.
- Using pictures and models to support their explanations.
- Reinforcing key ideas at every opportunity in other science topics.

These are all strategies that will be explored in later chapters.

Fixed mindset

Carol Dweck proposes that people have a tendency for either fixed or growth mindset thinking, but in reality we are probably all a combination of both. You could have a predominant growth mindset in one area but there can still be things that trigger you into fixed mindset thinking.[6] A fixed mindset means that students believe their intelligence is fixed and cannot be developed. A growth mindset means that students believe their intelligence can be developed through hard work and effort. In terms of our subject, a number of students hold the belief that they are 'not very good at science'. If you add to this the dreadful gender stereotypes that exist (e.g. 'boys are better at physics than girls') then we have a big problem. Dispelling these myths is a significant challenge for science teachers. If we are going to challenge students and raise their aspirations of what they can achieve, the first step is to make them believe that this is possible.

6 Carol Dweck, *Mindset: Changing the Way You Think to Fulfil Your Potential* (London: Robinson, 2006).

Misconceptions

Over the years, students will have picked up a number of incorrect 'facts' based on inaccurate scientific thinking and understanding; this is a huge issue for science teachers, as these mistakes compound misunderstanding when we try to develop their thinking further. For example, if a student believes that heat simply rises then they will not be able to understand the idea of convection currents, as they will not link heat transfer to changes in the density of the fluid. Scientific misconceptions are picked up and embedded all around us (e.g. we go to a supermarket and 'weigh' something in kilograms instead of newtons). This hinders our explanations. We need to identify and unpick these misunderstandings before we can build up and develop their knowledge.

Subject knowledge

Most science teachers who teach in the UK will be expected to teach biology, chemistry and physics, even though they will likely have specialised in only one of these disciplines during their higher education. The Sutton Trust's 2014 report, *What Makes Great Teaching?*, lists subject knowledge as one of the main characteristics of great teaching.[7] This presents a dilemma for science teachers. How can we stretch and challenge all students, through effective questioning and modelling, when we are teaching outside of our specialism?

---

7 Robert Coe, Cesare Aloisi, Steve Higgins and Lee Elliott Major, *What Makes Great Teaching? Review of the Underpinning Research*. Project Report (London: Sutton Trust, 2014). Available at: http://www.suttontrust.com/wp-content/uploads/2014/10/What-makes-teaching-great-FINAL-4.11.14.pdf.

With this in mind, there are two aspects of subject knowledge that need development and attention for science teachers:

1. The confusion over what we mean by 'subject knowledge for teaching'. This is generally understood as:
    - A detailed factual knowledge of our subject.
    - A deep understanding of theories in the subject, along with the frameworks for explaining these theories.
    - The ability to identify and address misconceptions.
    - An understanding of subject-specific skills.
    - A commitment to learning about new developments in the world of science.
2. When teaching outside of our science specialism, the following are likely to be true, unless we act to address them:
    - Subject knowledge will be less robust.
    - The range of stories to support explanations will be limited.
    - The teacher will bring their own misconceptions into play, and will be more likely to miss pupil misconceptions.
    - There will be less challenge through less effective questioning and modelling.

It's not just about the science

As well as teaching students scientific knowledge and skills, we have to teach a number of other interdisciplinary skills. For example, we have to teach them how to articulate their scientific ideas in well-written extended prose. We also have to teach them how to manipulate scientific formulae, analyse and interpret data and carry out complex mathematical calculations. If we are going to do this effectively, we need to be in tune with how the English and maths departments are teaching students. Furthermore, as practical work is a key element of science teaching, we also need to be up to date with health and safety regulations and make sure that these are implemented rigorously.

Knowledge of students

The students we teach (the frequency of shared classes in UK science departments, combined with the fact that it is a core subject, means that UK science teachers teach a lot of students) will have a wide range of scientific understanding. Consequently, science teachers need to be able to think carefully about how to stretch and challenge all students through effective delivery, questioning and feedback. How do you scaffold your questioning to ensure that students with a low starting point feel confident and are able to develop their responses, while those with a high starting point are sufficiently challenged and moved on? Similarly, what is the most effective way to give feedback to students that is both purposeful in terms of learning and manageable in terms of workload?

While the six pedagogical principles provide a framework for great teaching, great teachers need to be great at teaching their subject. This means they have to understand the challenges of implementing these principles within the context of their subject area. Only then can they develop their approach to teaching to overcome these challenges and so become experts at teaching their subject. That is the purpose of this book: to help all science teachers reflect on the challenges of implementing the six pedagogical principles in their own classrooms, and provide them with evidence-informed, gimmick-free and manageable classroom strategies that they can try out to make every science lesson count.

I started this introduction with a quote from a great science teacher, Pam McCulloch, and I'll finish with a quote about another. Ted Clarke was one of the inspirations behind our original book, *Making Every Lesson Count*, and he taught my wife, Lianne, chemistry in the 1980s in Porthcawl, South Wales. When I asked Lianne why Mr Clarke was such an impressive chemistry teacher she said:

> *Mr Clarke was and still is an inspiration to me. He is the best teacher I have ever had. He always set the bar of expectation high and expected all students to work hard, put the effort in and get there, irrespective of their ability. Low standards or excuses were not accepted! He made it his business to find out what you knew and what you didn't know and then guided you to get better and better – beyond what you thought was possible. Most importantly, though, he loved chemistry and cared deeply about every student he taught – his love of this subject became infectious.*

A truly inspirational teacher who brought his passion for science alive in every lesson. I hope this book has a similar effect! In each chapter you will find a number of practical teaching strategies designed to help you reflect on your teaching and bring the six principles to life. Nevertheless, all schools and classes are different, so it is up to you to refine them to suit your group and the topic you are teaching. After all, you are the expert in your classroom with your students.

So, let's get started!

Chapter 1
Challenge

Challenge can be described as the provision of difficult work that causes students to think deeply and engage in healthy struggle. This can be problematic for all teachers but there are particular issues that make this especially difficult for science teachers. During any one lesson, science teachers will have up to thirty students in their laboratory, all of whom will have different prior knowledge of scientific ideas, different levels of understanding of the scientific ideas being explored and different scientific misconceptions. Alongside this, their level of interest in the subject will also vary widely, ranging from the super-keen science fanatic, who has always been fascinated by dinosaurs, the solar system and exciting chemical reactions, to the surly teenager who appears to have a complete aversion to the subject. It is our job to synthesise all of this information and then push each student just enough to keep them in the struggle zone.

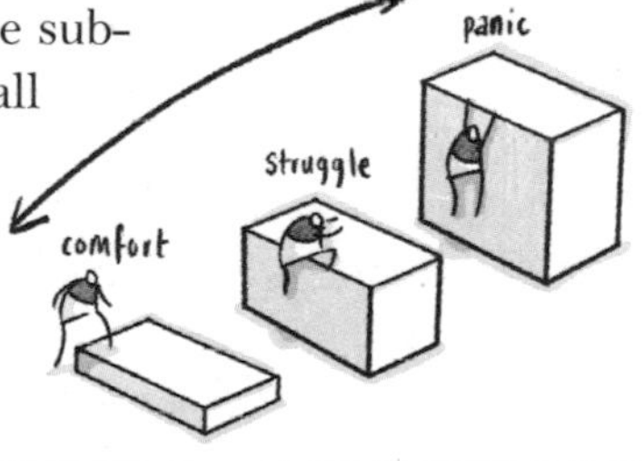

Comfort zone	Struggle zone	Panic zone
Low challenge. Low stress. Limited thinking. Limited learning.	High challenge. Low stress. Thinking required. Effective learning.	Very high challenge. High stress. Cognitive overload. Limited learning.

Challenge is slightly different from the other five principles. While there are specific teaching strategies that can be employed to ensure that challenge is appropriate for all the students we teach, the principle is more about an approach to teaching. Challenge is a long-term venture and should run through everything we do as science teachers – like the lettering that runs through a stick of rock. It's about the culture that we create in our science laboratories and the expectations that we have of the students we teach. The objective is always to try to keep students in the struggle zone, as shown in the previous diagram. This requires students to be thinking hard enough to support learning, but not so much that they reach cognitive overload and slip into the panic zone, where learning will be limited. Similarly, the work should not be easy, resulting in students remaining in the comfort zone.

The best science teachers create this culture by getting to know the students they teach, taking a genuine interest in their progress, making them believe that they can achieve beyond their own expectations and then supporting them – through the other five principles – to meet these expectations. Their science laboratories are places of interest, warmth and safe challenge where students feel secure enough to push and challenge their own thinking.

So, let's explore some strategies that we can put in place to start growing this culture.

Challenge Strategies

1. Curriculum first

Our starting point as secondary science teachers should be a challenging and interesting curriculum. We should scale up our Key Stage 3 curriculum to ensure that students are being exposed to challenging material – for example, rather than simply teaching students about particles in Year 7, why not teach them about subatomic particles and the arrangement of electrons in shells? Provided that we scaffold their learning carefully, most students will rise to the challenge and enjoy being exposed to these difficult ideas.

When asked to describe what he had been learning about in science, Jude, a Year 7 student at Durrington High School, responded:

We had a great science lesson today. Mr Canavan was telling us about subatomic particles. Electrons move around the outside of the atom in shells – shells are like lanes on a running track – the first shell holds two electrons, but then the others hold eight. They orbit the nucleus, which contains protons and neutrons. Protons have a positive charge and neutrons have a neutral charge. The electrons have a negative charge.

This student response, while perhaps not perfect, simply wouldn't have been possible if the science department at the school hadn't reviewed their Key Stage 3 curriculum and scaled up the content. The important point is that the students are being exposed to more demanding ideas. The challenge is then to do the same at GCSE level in Key Stage 4. By exposing students to material that is just beyond the expected level of the GCSE specification, the hardest content they will be exposed to will make the hardest content they have to remember for the exam seem easier by comparison.

2. Talk like a scientist

When thinking about vocabulary, we should consider the three different levels of words, as outlined by Dr Isabel Beck:[1]

- Tier 1 – high-frequency words, including objects and adjectives. These are rarely taught in school as they tend to be acquired preschool (e.g. book, chair).
- Tier 2 – cross curricular and often descriptive. Usually these can be explained using easier and more familiar words – for example, 'fortunate' is a more mature way of describing being lucky. These are words that are useful across subjects and in various situations (e.g. variables, method, theory, structure, interpretation). Students are likely to encounter these words through exposure to written texts and are unlikely to come across them in day-to-day discussion.
- Tier 3 – low-frequency words. These are subject specific and are not encountered a great deal in everyday language; when they are, they tend to be particular to a subject (e.g. respiration, refraction, molecule). If students don't understand the meaning of these words, and so can't use them appropriately, their academic achievement will be limited.

1 Isabel L. Beck, Margaret G. McKeown and Linda Kucan, *Bringing Words to Life: Robust Vocabulary Instruction* (New York: Guilford Press, 2002).

Language has important implications for science teachers. First, we need to explicitly teach the subtle differences in meaning of a tier 2 word in a science context compared to its use elsewhere. For instance, the students' experience of 'variable' would mean that something is or has been changing (e.g. "The weather has been highly variable this week"). In science, however, it has a more specific meaning. It is a factor in a science experiment that could change, but we either choose to keep the same measure or change it. Second, we need to expose them to tier 3 scientific vocabulary on a regular basis and repetitively. So rather than dumbing down our language (e.g. "The oil became more runny when it was heated"), we need to expose students to and teach them the correct meaning and use of scientific vocabulary (e.g. "As the oil was heated it had a lower viscosity, and so moved down the tile at a faster speed"). Having taught them tier 3 language, we then need to insist that they use it. Senior leader and education consultant Chris Moyse does this brilliantly by providing this poster for science teachers to put up on the walls of their laboratories:[2]

2 Chris Moyse, Talk Like … Resources (28 March 2016). Available at: https://chrismoyse.wordpress.com/2016/03/28/talk-like-resources/.

3. Surface then deep

John Hattie refers to the skill which means expert teachers know when to advance from surface learning to deep learning.[3] Surface learning is about knowing the key facts, whereas deep learning is about knowing how to relate, link and extend this knowledge. A common mistake that science teachers make is moving on to the deep learning before students have mastered the surface learning – the key knowledge that they need to master that topic. For example, before students can understand the idea of ionic bonding or covalent bonding (deep learning) they need to have a good understanding of atomic structure (surface learning). Atomic structure is the threshold concept. If they don't understand this, they cannot get to a profound understanding of ionic and covalent bonding. However, simple descriptions of ionic or covalent bonding could also be viewed as surface learning because simply talking about the 'sharing or transfer of electrons' does not really demonstrate deep learning. Deep learning would involve understanding bond breaking and bond making plus the energy changes involved. As science teachers we need to make sure students are clear on the surface learning before going deep, and that we are clear about what we expect of them in terms of deep learning. We can do this in a number of ways, such as hinge questions, quizzes or a simple question and answer session. It needs to be an essential part of our planning.

3 Hattie, The Science of Learning.

4. Think now

The anchor effect is one of the most robust findings in experimental psychology. In essence, it suggests that our perceptions are heavily influenced by the first piece of information we receive on a topic.[4] For example, if you see an antique piece of jewellery and an expert tells you it is worth £300, and you negotiate a price of £250, you will think you have a good deal based on the first price you were given. In reality it might only be worth £50, but you have anchored your expectations around £300. This has very significant implications for the science teacher. We need to ensure that the first thing students see and think about when they enter the science laboratory is challenging and will make them think. This will anchor in challenge from the start of the lesson, and as a consequence their perception of success from this point on will be based around this objective. Having a 'think now' task ready at the start of the lesson can help to achieve this. This can take a variety of forms:

- A picture to promote thinking (e.g. a picture of different specialised cells with the students asked to describe and explain how the structure of each one helps it to do its job).
- A photo to promote thinking about a scientific issue (e.g. trees killed by acid rain, a parachutist descending to illustrate the forces acting on a falling object).
- A difficult question that will stimulate thinking.

As well as promoting thinking and anchoring in challenge from the beginning, 'think now' tasks are also useful in terms of ensuring a calm and purposeful start to lessons.

4 Daniel Kahneman, *Thinking, Fast and Slow* [Kindle edn] (London: Allen Lane, 2011), loc. 1998–2180.

5. Think hard

Consider the following questions that might be asked in a science lesson:

Why do we need carbohydrates and fats in our diet?

Most students would be able to recall that these two are important because they release energy.

Why do we need protein in our diet?

Again – no problem. Most students would know that this is for growth and repair. Then there is this question:

What is the link between carbohydrates and protein in our diet?

A number of students will struggle with this. They will find it hard to link the two ideas – that is, the energy released from carbohydrates is used to build proteins for growth and repair. So, going back to Hattie, their surface learning is secure but their deep learning isn't.

What can we do about this? Plan into our lessons a 'think hard' question. This is a question (or series of questions) that will require the students to think hard and make connections between ideas. More importantly, we should make it explicit that it's a 'think hard' question by telling the students so or, for example, using a distinctive graphic on the PowerPoint slide along with the question.

Clearly, this is a pre-planned question that we should expect the students to respond to in writing. This is different from the verbal questioning that takes place all of the time in lessons, which can't be planned for as it is usually framed around student responses (and we all know how unpredictable they can be!). Obviously, by doing more structured 'think hard' questions like this more frequently, the requirement for them to be thinking deeply should help their learning. It will also provide our brightest students with a regular diet of challenging questions.

It's important to make these questions explicit for a number of reasons:

- By telling students it's hard, we are also telling them that it's going to be okay to struggle with this – in fact, we'll struggle with it together and it will be alright!
- Focusing on these 'think hard' questions in our planning will make us think about the surface learning that will need to be embedded in order for the students to answer them, so we should be more aware of the surface to deep tipping point.
- Experiencing success with these challenging questions will support their intrinsic motivation. Students don't just get motivated because we tell them to; they are motivated when they experience success and want to build on this further.

6. Success narratives

If we really want to challenge students and set the bar of expectation high, we should do this from the first lesson in September. Save the best exercise books from your most successful students at the end of Year 11 and show them to the students who are embarking on their GCSE course in Year 10. Use these books to point out the features of successful work. This might include:

- Neatly presented work.
- Well-organised work with titles underlined.
- Diagrams drawn with a pencil and ruler.
- Fully labelled tables, diagrams and graphs.
- Experiments written up in a common format in line with scientific convention.
- Feedback has been responded to appropriately.
- Detailed explanations and answers to questions.

You could even go a stage further and display these books in your science laboratory so they can be referred to on a regular basis. The other advantage of this is that it shows the students how to write in the science genre. As scientists we often take this for granted, but many students won't have seen an experiment written up in the correct way before (e.g.

introduction, prediction, diagram, method, results table, conclusion and evaluation). Showing them model examples sets the standard for them to aspire to, and it also shows them what can be achieved with hard work and effort.

7. Struggle plenary

If we are being honest, most of us would confess to having carried out a plenary that goes something along the lines of, "So what have we learnt today?" or even worse, "Well done today – we have all learnt the structure and function of the parts of an animal and plant cell." The first is problematic because they won't have *learnt* anything in one lesson. They might be able to *recall* it, but you will only know if they have learnt it if they can still tell you about it in a week or a month's time. The second is worse because you are simply telling them what *you* have covered! A much better approach is to ask them what they have struggled with in the lesson. This supports the idea of growing a culture of challenge, as you are making it okay to talk about and embrace struggle.

This is key for science teachers. Much of what we teach works at a number of levels, again linking back to the idea of surface and deep learning. So, while students might be able to label the different parts of a cell, can they really explain the function of each of the organelles? Furthermore, can they explain how the organelles interact to ensure the functioning of the whole cell? If not, then this should inform your planning for next lesson. Students might be reticent about doing this to start with. Overcome this by using phrases such as, "When I was at school I found X really tricky to understand. How did you do with it today?"

Reflective Questions

- How do you ensure that your subject knowledge, across the scientific disciplines that you teach, is strong enough to stretch and challenge all students?
- How do you ensure that you know the strengths and weaknesses of the students you teach so that you are able to keep all of them in the struggle zone?
- Are you confident answering the hardest questions that the students you teach will have to answer?
- Do you insist on scientific academic language at all times?
- Do you plan 'think hard' questions that will stretch your students and make them link complex ideas together?
- How do you get your students thinking from the start of the lesson?
- Do you encourage a culture of struggle and challenge by asking the students what they have struggled with each lesson?

Chapter 2

Explanation

Explanation is the bread and butter of science teachers. As scientists, we have a large body of scientific ideas that we know and understand and we have to transfer that understanding to our students. Many of these ideas are abstract and complex. Furthermore, the students will also have a wide range of misconceptions that will need to be unpicked before we can begin to successfully build and develop new knowledge.

When thinking about our explanations, there are four questions that science teachers should consider:

1 How do we tether new knowledge to what students already know? Psychologists refer to the framework of things we know – our store of knowledge – and how we organise new information as a schema. It is widely accepted in cognitive science that we are more likely to absorb new knowledge if it links to existing schemata. For example, if students already have a good understanding of the particle nature of matter, they are more

likely to be able to explain changes of state such as evaporation and condensation.

2 How can we introduce new ideas in clear steps? We know from cognitive science that the working memory (the part of our cognitive system that holds, processes and manipulates information) has a limit to what it can do – known as cognitive load.[1] If we try to present too much information to students at once, there is a real risk that we will overload their working memory, resulting in confusion and a lack of processing.

3 How do we avoid the curse of the expert? As scientists we are experts who are teaching novices, our students. This brings with it a real problem – the curse of the expert. We have to be incredibly careful when explaining new ideas not to ignore knowledge that we have (and take for granted) that our students will not have. For example, when talking about gas exchange in the lungs, we are assuming that students know about diffusion, ventilation of the lungs and the structure of the alveoli. If they don't, they will struggle to fully understand gas exchange.

4 How do we make abstract ideas concrete? This is linked to the curse of the expert. We need to think carefully about how we can make abstract scientific ideas (e.g. diffusion of gases, changes of state, chemical reactions) concrete and tangible to students.

---

1 See John Sweller, Cognitive Load Theory, Learning Difficulty, and Instructional Design, *Learning and Instruction* 4 (1994): 295–312. Available at: http://www.realtechsupport.org/UB/I2C/Sweller_CognitiveLoadTheory_1994.pdf.

Explanation Strategies

By answering these questions we arrive at the four principles of explanation that we are looking to achieve; we should now explore what we can do in our science laboratories to put them into action.

1. Science stories

As humans, we are hard-wired from an evolutionary point of view to learn new knowledge through storytelling. This is how our ancestors have passed on their wisdom to the younger generations for thousands of years. This is great news for scientists as we have a plethora of stories available to us to help explain scientific ideas. As science teachers we should make it our business to know the history of the science we are teaching and use this to enhance our explanations with stories. For example:

- Antiseptic: tell the story of how Ignaz Semmelweis observed that the incidence of puerperal fever in maternity wards could be drastically reduced by hand disinfection.

- Extinction: the obvious story to tell here is the mass extinction of the dinosaurs and the Alvarez hypothesis – the theory of an asteroid collision on earth and associated climate change. Similarly, the extinction of the dodo, due to hunting by human explorers, is another story that students find irresistible.
- Falling objects: when discussing the influence of air resistance on falling objects, tell the story of the astronaut David Scott on *Apollo 15* and how he dropped a hammer and a feather on the surface of the moon. As the only force acting on them was the moon's gravity, they both fell with the same acceleration.

Stories work because they take very complex ideas and put them into a very real context that students can understand. The human nature of the stories makes them highly memorable for the students.

2. Find the sweet spot

As described at the start of this chapter, new knowledge needs to be built upon existing knowledge or schemata. In order to do this we need to find out what the students already know. Alongside this, though, it is just as important to find out what misconceptions the students may have, as these will make it harder to progress their understanding. We need to find the 'sweet spot' – that is, what they know that is helpful, what they know that is not helpful and how we can build on that. This should inform where you pitch your explanation.

There are a number of ways we can do this:

- **"Tell me what you know about …"** Very simply, ask the students to either tell you or write a paragraph about the new topic. Writing a whole paragraph about a new topic can be difficult, so this idea could be developed along the lines of, "Write down ten facts you know about radioactivity."

- **Visual prompt.** Introduce a new topic by showing the students an image that links to the topic and then questioning them on it. For example, when introducing the digestive system, show them a diagram and question them about it (e.g. What is each part of the digestive system called? What does each part do? Why is it important?).
- **Demonstration prompt.** This is similar to the visual prompt. Show students a practical demonstration and then use this to probe their understanding of the topic. For example, when introducing the idea of chemical reactions, carry out a simple reaction such as burning magnesium ribbon in air, show students the resulting product (magnesium oxide) and then probe them about what has happened through questioning (e.g. How is the magnesium oxide different from the magnesium? How was this formed? Why did we need to heat it? Why was there a bright flash? Could we easily get the magnesium back? Why do we call this an oxidation reaction?). It is clear how this kind of questioning following a practical demonstration will provide you with a wealth of information about what they know about the topic.
- **Straight to the point.** Rather than waiting for the students to reveal their misconceptions about science, you can probably second guess them and unpick them early on. For example, when looking at the expansion of solids during heating, the students would probably provide you with the following explanations:
    - The particles get bigger when heated, so take up more space.
    - The particles vibrate more because they have more energy, so take up more space.

◊ The particles react with the heat and make more particles, which then take up more space.

These are all pretty standard responses, so why not present them to the students straight away and discuss with them which one is right and why the others aren't? In this way, you are not relying on them to reveal their erroneous beliefs but making them explicit from the start.

- **Concept cartoons.** Brenda Keogh and Stuart Naylor have produced a series of simple cartoons that present students with their own misconceptions about key scientific ideas.[2] These can be presented to the students and then used to generate discussion and elicit what they do and don't know about a topic. You can then give pointers about how their ideas might be further developed.

3. Open the curiosity gap

Young people are naturally curious – like all young animals, curiosity is how they learn to navigate and survive in the world around them. As science teachers, we can use this to our advantage at the start of the lesson. Show the students

2 Brenda Keogh and Stuart Naylor, *Concept Cartoons in Science Education* (Sandbach: Millgate House Publishers, 2000).

something interesting that will make them curious about the topic and keen to find out more (e.g. an artery that has become blocked by fatty material, the aftermath of the nuclear explosion at Chernobyl, a video of a textile impregnated with nanoparticles that repel water). Following this, explain to them that by the end of the lesson they will be able to explain what they have seen. Their natural inquisitiveness should make them want to fill the curiosity gap that you have opened.

4. Make the abstract concrete

As scientists we deal with abstract concepts all the time – for example, the flow of electricity, the structure of the atom, the particle nature of matter, cells and chemical reactions. These are all things the students can't actually see, so they need to be able to visualise them if they are going to genuinely understand them. So how can we make these concepts more concrete?

- **Practical demonstrations and experiments.** This is the most obvious tool that science teachers have at their disposal. For example, understanding convection as a purely theoretical model is conceptually difficult. However, if the students are shown a demonstration – such as the 'model mine' with smoke being carried up and down by the convection currents in the air – it becomes more real, as long as it is supported with effective commentary and questioning.
- **Link it to what they already know.** Sticking with convection, most students will know about hot air balloons, or that it's often warmer upstairs than it is downstairs, or that Christmas decorations above radiators will often flutter. Unpick with them why this is (i.e. because hot air rises). Now that you have made this idea concrete you can then go on to look at the theoretical explanation as to

why this happens. Similarly, when introducing static electricity, ask the students how many of them have rubbed a balloon on their hair and then stuck it to the wall!

- **Use models.** A model is a representation of an idea, object, process or system that is used to describe and explain phenomena that cannot be experienced directly. The flow of an electric current is conceptually difficult, so is a good example of where a model can be used to support understanding. If the students don't understand the basics of electron flow they will struggle to understand ideas such as series and parallel circuits, resistance and voltage. Link this to a model that they will be familiar with, such as the hot water system that heats their house (i.e. the boiler and pump push hot water around the pipes to the radiators, where heat energy is then dissipated), as most students will understand this. In a similar way, a battery provides the 'push' for electrons to flow in the wire, with their energy being transferred at devices such as light bulbs. As well as to understand processes, models can also be used to explain scale in science. For example, the size of the nucleus of an atom could be compared to a marble in the centre circle of a football stadium, with the stadium representing the size of the atom and a grain of rice in the stands of the stadium an electron.

  It is important to understand that models also have limitations. If not discussed appropriately they can support and embed misconceptions. For example, a clear plastic bag with a ball inside it is often used to represent an animal cell. The plastic bag signifies the cell membrane, the inside of the bag the cytoplasm and the ball the nucleus. While this supports certain aspects of cell structure (e.g. the flexible nature of the cell membrane, the cell membrane as a barrier between the inside and outside of the cell), it has some clear limitations. The cell membrane is not a solid lining like plastic; it is fluid and dynamic. In fact, the best way to model a cell membrane is to pour some vegetable oil into water and observe it float on the surface. The oil layer is far more representative of the cell membrane than a plastic bag is.

- **Make it about them.** Try to make concepts relevant and important to the students as individuals. A great one for this is when looking at cells. It's one thing looking at a diagram of cells in a book or at a pre-prepared slide under the microscope; however, nothing will beat a student preparing and observing actual onion cells or, even better, one of their own cheek cells! This really does make the concept of cells come alive and have real meaning.

5. Explain and probe

When science teachers are explaining new ideas, we do need to explicitly tell students about them in order to share our knowledge. There is nothing wrong with this and, contrary to some recent thinking in education, we shouldn't be ashamed of this 'teacher talk'. We know stuff and they don't, so we have to tell them!

However, the best science teachers are very skilled at punctuating their explanations with questioning and modelling. While specific strategies for questioning and modelling are discussed within the relevant chapters, it is important to also mention their role in explanations. For example, when explaining a concept such as terminal velocity we can use a range of questions to shape and develop students' understanding of our explanation (e.g. What are the two forces acting on a falling object? Which one is greatest to start with? Why does air resistance increase as the speed increases? What will eventually happen to the two forces? What will this do to the speed?). At the same time, you can use a range of visual prompts to support their understanding – from simply dropping an object to illustrate the motion to showing them a clip of a parachutist.

The principle here should be applied to all explanations: shape your explanation and the students' understanding by asking them questions and modelling what you are talking about during the process of explaining.

6. Repeat the key learning points

It's really important that during your planning you are very clear about the key learning points that you want the students to understand – for instance, how mutation, adaptation and natural selection result in evolution, using collision theory to explain how different factors affect the rate of a chemical reaction, or how the forces acting on a falling object affect the motion of an object.

Following our initial explanation of this key learning during the lesson, we should not just leave it there. We should come back to the fundamental learning points at different phases of the lesson, and indeed in future lessons when it links to a related topic and the concept naturally fits in. This enables us to embed these crucial ideas. For example:

- When planning how to answer an exam question (e.g. What's the key learning point we need to use in order to answer this question?).
- Following a practical (e.g. What's the key learning point we need to use in order to explain the trends we have observed in the results of this practical?).

7. Make practical work meaningful

Practical work should not simply be something the students do to occupy their time in science lessons. It should have one of three purposes:

1 To illustrate a scientific idea (e.g. reacting elements such as magnesium and oxygen to form a compound such as magnesium oxide).

2 To develop skills and techniques (e.g. using a microscope or carrying out titration).

3 To investigate relationships and test out ideas/questions (e.g. does increasing the temperature affect the rate of a chemical reaction?).

One overriding purpose of practical work is to help students understand scientific ideas and support the explanations they have received in lessons. We need to proceed with caution though. If students don't have a strong knowledge of, for example, atoms, ions and the principles of electrolysis, then they won't gain a great deal from a practical where they carry out the electrolysis of a salt solution. They will just follow a set of instructions with very little understanding about why they are doing so.

The evidence suggests that practical work is often surprisingly limited in terms of students gaining an understanding of scientific ideas: "Practical work was generally effective in getting students to do what is intended with physical objects, but much less effective in getting them to use the intended scientific ideas to guide their actions and reflect upon the data they collect."[3] So, if you are using practical work to embed and support your explanations, make sure the students are secure with the knowledge linked to the practical beforehand so the practical work has a clear context.

Furthermore, don't necessarily expect the students to use practical work to develop their scientific knowledge and understanding. This is counter-intuitive to what most science teachers believe to be the case – we think it will help students to 'find out about science'. It probably won't. It would appear that the strongest outcome of practical work is to make students more adept at using scientific apparatus.

We should consider the two elements of practical work: the complexity of the procedure and the complexity of the scientific ideas behind it. If the complexity levels of both are too high, because we have to explain both, then there is a risk that the students will be overloaded, and as a result acquire only a limited degree of learning from the practical. Similarly, if the complexity levels of both are too low, then the purpose of the exercise is questionable. The trick is to find the sweet spot, where the complexity of both the practical procedure and the scientific ideas being explored is just enough to keep students in the struggle zone.

---

3 Ian Abrahams and Robin Millar, Does Practical Work Really Work? A Study of the Effectiveness of Practical Work as a Teaching and Learning Method in School Science, *International Journal of Science Education* 30(14) (2008): 1945–1969 at 1945.

8. Build your explanation

In Chapter 1 we discussed Hattie's idea of surface and deep learning. This has important implications for science teachers when planning their explanations. All too often we move too quickly through these – that is, we don't make sure that the students are secure with the surface learning before moving on to the deep learning.

Consider the process of understanding the properties of a giant ionic lattice such as sodium chloride. In order to grasp this the students will need to be secure with the following concepts beforehand:

- Atomic structure
- Properties of subatomic particles
- How atoms become ions
- How ions have different charges
- Electrostatic forces of attraction
- How ions form ionic bonds
- What we mean by an electric current
- The difference between melting and dissolving

If any one of these essential pieces of knowledge is missing, the students will struggle to fully understand and explain the properties of giant ionic lattices. Hence, we need to consider in our planning what knowledge the students will need from our explanation in order to fully understand the more demanding work. This is equally important for science curriculum leaders when planning long-term schemes of work.

9. Be an expert

As discussed in the Introduction, the Sutton Trust report, *What Makes Great Teaching?*, ranks subject knowledge as the top contributory factor to great teaching. This can be problematic for science teachers as most of us have to also teach outside of our specialism of biology, chemistry or physics. A biology graduate will undoubtedly feel very confident teaching biology to even the brightest students. They will feel able to extend their understanding, respond to their questions and add a rich breadth and depth to their explanations. They are less likely to feel this way about teaching chemistry or physics.

Rebecca Owen, a science teacher at Durrington High School, sums this up well:

As a relatively new teacher, I was teaching lots of physics classes (my specialism was biology) and a number of students in these classes were very bright. I felt uncomfortable with my explanations of tricky abstract concepts as I didn't know all of the science behind the topics I was teaching. As a result, I felt very insecure teaching topics that I hadn't covered myself for a number of years. I was covering the basics, but felt unable to really push the students and felt anxious when they came across difficult questions. I felt that my students were not getting a good deal – which frustrated me professionally because I really cared about their progress. It's difficult to enthuse students if you don't love your subject. You've got be passionate about your subject and be in love with it if you're going to teach it well!

We need to make it our business to develop our subject knowledge across all of the scientific disciplines we teach. Rebecca decided to tackle this head on and proactively addressed her own subject knowledge in the following ways:

- Use the expertise of colleagues. How do they teach the topic? What are the best practicals to use? What do students find hard? What misconceptions do they have? How do they overcome this? Not only did Rebecca use the expertise of colleagues within her own team but she also used the support of coaches from the Institute of Physics.
- Observe colleagues. Watch the subject experts teach the really difficult topics.
- Know the specification inside out. Make it your business to fully scrutinise every aspect of the specification.
- Look at exam papers, sit them yourself and then mark them using the mark scheme. Identify your own knowledge gaps and fill them.
- Use scientific books, journals and websites to read around the subject so that you can add the same richness to all topics.
- Practise your explanations with a subject expert and ask them for feedback.
- Practise any unfamiliar practicals or demonstrations beforehand and make sure you can explain all aspects of them fully.

Two years on, Rebecca now gets some of the best physics GCSE results in the school!

Don't compromise on the quality of your explanations – make it your business to make them consistently excellent.

10. Words and visuals

When explaining key ideas, support your verbal explanation with visuals. Describing something like the structure of an atom using words alone can be quite confusing for the students due to the abstract nature of the concept. By using a visual you are condensing a great deal of information into one image and so focusing attention more clearly. Furthermore, when relying solely on text the students will have to use their working memory to store the bits of information you are imparting, and this may soon become too much. This can be avoided by using visuals on the board – either prepared on a PowerPoint or drawn yourself – to support your explanation. Visuals minimise the cognitive load on students as they are quicker and easier to process than lines of text.

By using diagrams in this way you are also making it easier for the students to memorise information. Visuals act as triggers for memory and provide a framework for new knowledge to be hooked onto. It also stops the class formulating misconceptions, as what you say could be easily misinterpreted by different students. This is less likely if they can all see the same diagram.

11. Links to the big ideas

Science should not be viewed as a group of disparate ideas which don't link together. Everything we teach students should be 'glued together' by the big ideas in science. Wynne Harlen has identified ten 'big ideas in science' that serve as a good framework:[4]

1 All matter in the universe is made of very small particles.

4 Wynne Harlen (ed.), *Working with Big Ideas in Science Education* (Trieste: Science Education Programme, 2015). Available at: http://www.ase.org.uk/documents/working-with-the-big-ideas-in-science-education/, pp. 15–16.

2 Objects can affect other objects at a distance.

3 Changing the movement of an object requires a net force to be acting on it.

4 The total amount of energy in the universe is always the same but can be transferred from one energy store to another during an event.

5 The composition of the earth and its atmosphere and the processes occurring within them shape the earth's surface and its climate.

6 Our solar system is a very small part of one of billions of galaxies in the universe.

7 Organisms are organised on a cellular basis and have a finite life span.

8 Organisms require a supply of energy and materials for which they often depend on, or compete with, other organisms.

9 Genetic information is passed down from one generation of organisms to another.

10 The diversity of organisms, living and extinct, is the result of evolution.

A simpler version of the big ideas in science could be:

- Particles
- Forces
- Energy
- Cells
- Interdependence

Ideas that are connected are easier to use when the students are presented with new problems or ideas. Linking new topics, via these big ideas, makes it easier for students to understand the new topics and the ideas themselves. For example, when talking about conduction and convection you can relate this to particles. Similarly, when describing renewable and non-renewable power sources you can link this with energy. You can see how using the 'glue' of big ideas makes it easier for the students to understand these new topics.

Reflective Questions

- How do you find out the prior knowledge of the students you teach?
- How do you keep your scientific knowledge up to date, so that you are able to bring a contemporary scientific context to the material you teach?
- How do you ensure that your students are secure with the surface learning before moving on to the deep learning?
- How do you ensure that you 'chunk up' your explanations so as to not overload students?
- How do you punctuate your explanations with questions and modelling?

Chapter 3
Modelling

Having explained complicated scientific ideas and skills to the students, they need to know what to do with these in order to come up with a 'product'. They need to watch and listen to an expert (i.e. their science teacher) who will guide them through the process step by step before they attempt to do it themselves. The challenge for science teachers is that the product we are modelling can be one of many things – for example:

- How to carry out a piece of practical work.
- How to write up a report of an experiment.
- How to communicate our scientific ideas through writing or drawing.
- How to analyse and interpret data.
- How to use and manipulate scientific formulae to carry out calculations.
- How to apply our knowledge to unfamiliar situations.

It's worth considering some of the issues concerned with each of these in turn before we think about strategies that can be used to address them.

How to carry out a piece of practical work

When it comes to secondary science lessons, students will be using laboratory equipment that they won't have come across before to perform techniques that they won't have carried out before. With this in mind, you will need to take care that you precisely model how to use the apparatus and the steps involved in the practical work – don't assume that they will know any of the steps in the procedure. Not only will this ensure that the students get the best out of the practical work, but it will also ensure that they work safely.

When practical work is not modelled well to students before they start work themselves, the following outcomes are all possible:

- Students injuring themselves or somebody else.
- Students simply switching off and becoming bored because they don't know what to do.
- Students getting it wrong and then you having to spend a great deal of time correcting them.
- Students doing the experiment incorrectly and gathering worthless data that won't be useful to their learning.

Any one of these is bad enough, but when put together will make for a very difficult lesson.

Another consideration when modelling practical work is the idea of working memory – this is the brain's capacity to hold, manipulate and process information. It is generally agreed that the brain has the capacity to hold and process about seven elements at any one time.[1] This has implications

1 See George A. Miller, The Magical Number Seven, Plus or Minus Two: Some Limits on Our Capacity for Processing Information, *Psychological Review* 63(2) (1956): 81–97.

when giving instructions for practical work as most people would struggle to cope with more than five to nine steps at the same time.

If you are going to model practical work with students, you need to be able to do the work confidently yourself. If you are teaching a technique or process for the first time, it is essential that you practise it before it is undertaken with a class, irrespective of your teaching experience.

How to write up a report of an experiment

Students have to learn how to write in a number of different genres in secondary school because of the different subjects they study. A science graduate will be quite comfortable with the writing style required for a scientific experiment report but a teenager will not be – they will need to be explicitly taught how to write in this style. Furthermore, as we saw with tier 2 words in Chapter 1, they will need to learn how to use a number of words which they may already be familiar with but in a completely different context (e.g. accurate, precise, reliable).

How to communicate our scientific ideas through writing or drawing

Communicating scientific ideas is a key aspect of modelling for science teachers. Many scientific ideas are very complex and abstract – for instance, the structure of the atom and the features of subatomic particles. Understanding these ideas is hard enough for students, so we should never underestimate the challenges students face when they are asked to describe and explain these complex ideas in writing, whether that is as part of an exercise during a lesson or when writing an extended answer to an exam question.

How to analyse and interpret data

Analysing and interpreting data is an essential aspect of the work of any scientist. And there is a great deal to it: collecting data, recording it in tables, analysing it, displaying it graphically, looking for trends and patterns, spotting any anomalous results, describing and explaining these trends and then using them to draw conclusions. Furthermore, each individual step is fraught with complexities for the average teenager. Graph drawing, for instance, can provide plenty of opportunities for error if not modelled correctly (e.g. getting the axes right, using the correct scales, including the units, plotting the points accurately, drawing a line/curve of best fit). An important issue for us as science teachers is to know something of the progression of mathematical ideas and how these are taught in our school – for example, drawing simple line graphs is pretty straightforward but progressing to lines of best fit is more challenging. In order to support your science teaching you should find out when and how these topics are taught in your school.

How to use and manipulate scientific formulae to carry out calculations

Applying and manipulating formulae to carry out calculations in science requires students to apply their mathematical skills to a different subject. This is not always easy for students because of the way we compartmentalise subjects in UK secondary schools. Students can be reluctant to transfer knowledge (e.g. how to rearrange equations) from one subject to another unless explicity prompted to do so. This might be compounded by the maths and science departments using different approaches to tackle the same kind of question. For example, science teachers will often use the 'triangle method' to rearrange formulae. While this will get students to the right answer, it won't aid their wider mathematical understanding. Furthermore, these calculations often have a number of stages to them that will need to be broken down and modelled. Again, a conversation with the maths department will help with this.

How to apply our knowledge to unfamiliar situations

Students really struggle with applying their current knowledge to novel scenarios. While they might have a great understanding of the process of photosynthesis and plant nutrition, if they are presented with an exam question that asks them about the optimal growing conditions required in a commercial tomato greenhouse, they will often struggle to use their knowledge of photosynthesis to answer the question. With this in mind, we need to model our own thinking process when we are tackling this kind of question. Thinking about thought processes is often referred to as metacognition.

It's clear that modelling is key to effective science teaching. More than that, though, the best science teachers need to be skilled at modelling a variety of different things to students.

Let's now consider some of the most effective modelling strategies that science teachers can use.

Modelling Strategies

1. Live modelling

When we want to model any kind of scientific writing to our students – whether it is an answer to an exam question, an experimental write-up or an extended piece of writing

– the best thing we can do is simply approach the whiteboard with a pen. All too often, the mistake that science teachers make is to simply show students a piece of writing or a model answer that they need to aspire to, without any attempt to show them how to produce it. While there is a place for showing exemplar pieces of writing via a PowerPoint, visualiser or similar, I think this is even more effective when combined with the teacher writing something on the board with the students.

The reason for this is simple. It allows you to discuss and explain how and why you are writing in the way that you are in order to get to the end product. It also allows you to get input from the students and, importantly, they will see you going wrong! This last point is crucial. If you just stand at the front and write out a perfect paragraph, this will have limited use for the students. Yes, they will see the finished result, but they won't actually have seen the process necessary to get there. If they see you making a mistake, and then you discuss with them why it's a mistake and how to correct it, that will be really powerful.

If you start by showing the students a model answer, make sure you unpick some key points with them first. For example:

- What is the question asking for (e.g. describe, explain, compare, analyse, evaluate)?
- What does each of these key terms mean?

- What key knowledge is required in order to answer the question?
- How and where has the writer used this knowledge in the answer? Highlight this key knowledge in the text.
- How have they answered the question (e.g. where have they *described* the trend and where have they *explained* it)?

Once you have worked backwards from the model response, then you can reverse the process – starting with a question and constructing the answer together using the points you have discussed when deconstructing the model answer.

Some prompts to consider sharing while you are live modelling include:

- What are the key scientific ideas that I need to be using in this answer/piece of writing?
- What is the question asking me?
- How am I going to structure this piece of writing?
- Why do you think I started the sentence in that way?
- What do you think the next sentence should be?
- What is a more scientifically accurate word to use for …?
- What do you think I mean by that?
- If you were going to finish this sentence, what would you write?
- What's wrong with that sentence?
- Have I included all of the key scientific points?
- Have I used appropriate scientific terminology?

Live modelling is key to developing strong scientific writing, and it's about more than just showing students a finished piece. It's about deconstructing it by discussing with them the thinking and the process which will get them there. Following this, it's about using this discussion to co-construct a piece of writing using what you have learnt from the initial deconstruction process. It's also a really important way of promoting effective questioning, as can be seen from the prompt questions.

So, the next time you plan to simply project a piece of writing up on the board and expect the students to emulate it, stop yourself. Talk about how the writer got there and then get your board pen out and start writing yourself!

2. Build the diagram

Consider this issue: you want to describe and explain how the structure of the small intestine is linked to the absorption of food molecules following digestion. While planning your lesson, you look on the Internet for a diagram of the small intestine and then copy and paste it into your PowerPoint slide. During your lesson, you come to this point of teaching and you show the students the illustration that, to you, makes perfect sense. To your surprise, they are completely confused and say it makes no sense to them. This is not terribly surprising and is the result of the expert, you, underestimating the complexities of a scientific diagram. The students won't understand the context of the image – that is, they won't understand where that tiny piece of the small intestine fits in with their existing knowledge of the intestine, which is a tube inside the abdomen.

This is where the trusty board pen comes in handy again. Use your artistic skills to build up the diagram yourself. It doesn't actually matter if you can't draw – in fact, in some ways, bad drawing is to be encouraged! The students will find it amusing and often more memorable: "Hey Miss, do you remember the time you tried to draw a small intestine and it looked like a wrinkly snake?" Start by drawing what they know (e.g. an outline of the abdomen). Then add in the shape of the small intestine. You can then use your questioning skills to build up the diagram – for example, "Where will the digested food be?" When they work out that it is inside the intestine, draw an enlarged cross-section of the intestine.

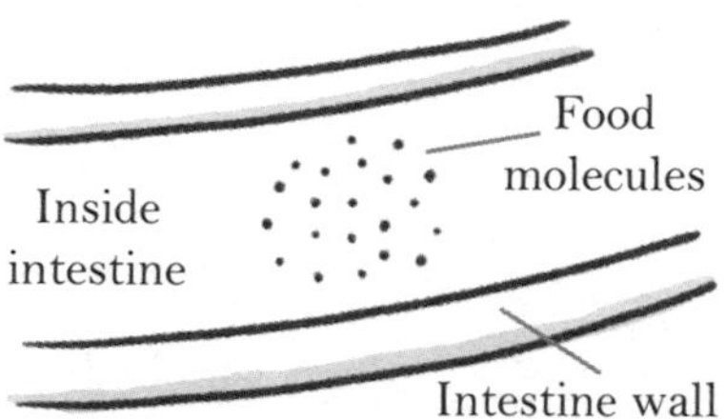

Notice that where possible the labelling is inside the diagram. Cognitive load theory suggests that this type of labelling helps students to remember the parts of a diagram as their eyes don't have to scan across it. Follow this with more questioning:

Teacher: Where does the food need to get to?

Student: The cells, Miss.

Teacher: Correct. How will it move there?

Student: In the blood.

At this point, add a blood vessel to the wall of your intestine. Don't be tempted to embed misconceptions here and draw the blood vessel outside of the intestine. While you are keeping it simple, you are also keeping it accurate.

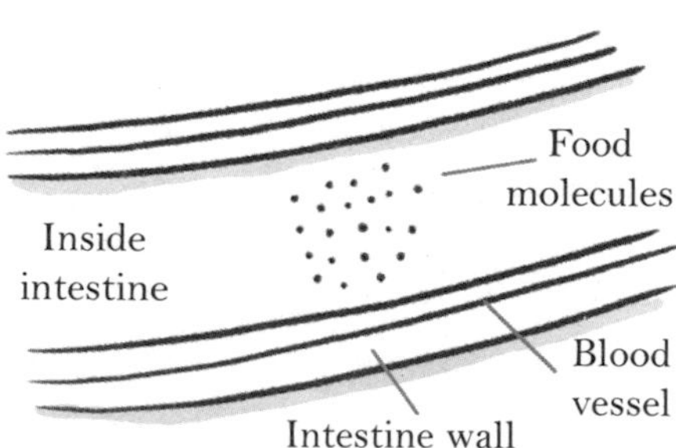

Then ask more questions:

Teacher: Correct. So if it's in the intestine and it needs to get into the blood vessel, what needs to happen?

Student: It needs to pass through the lining of the intestine and into the blood vessel.

Continue to question the students about how the lining of the intestine could be adapted to increase the rate of absorption across its surface until they start to get to the fact that folding the inner lining of the intestine could increase the rate of absorption. Then demonstrate this by adapting a section of your original diagram to show the villi:

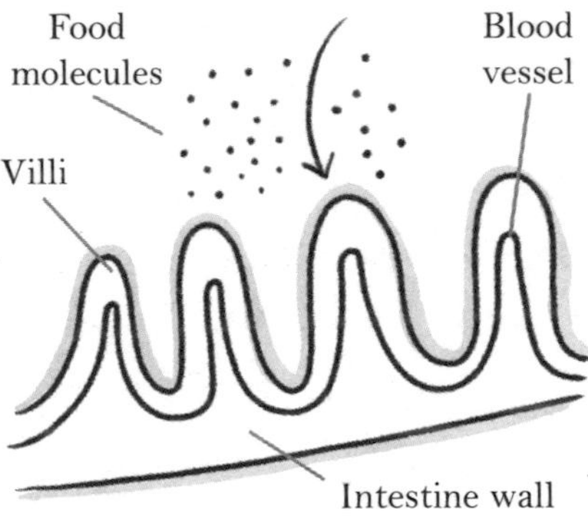

By gradually modelling the drawing of a diagram in this way, you will slowly build up the students' understanding of the structure. It's at this point that you could link your diagrams to other more sophisticated or out of context diagrams, as by now they should have a good idea of what the diagram is meant to demonstrate.

3. Comparative modelling

When we talk about comparative modelling, we mean showing students two examples of a piece of writing – one strong and one weak. If we are simply shown one example of a piece of writing or a diagram in isolation, it can be quite difficult to critique it. However, if we provide students with the opportunity to compare one model answer to another, we make it much easier for them to pick out the strengths and weaknesses of each one.

For example, if we showed students this answer to the question, "Describe and explain the structure of an atom," they may initially think that it is pretty good:

Student A:

An atom consists of a central nucleus containing protons and neutrons. The nucleus is orbited by electrons which travel around in shells.

However, when we show it next to this one they will spot the weaknesses in Student A's response:

Student B:

The nucleus of an atom contains protons and neutrons. Protons have a positive charge and neutrons have a neutral charge. Both of these particles have a mass of 1. Orbiting this central nucleus are electrons, in shells. The first shell can hold two electrons and then others will hold eight. Electrons have a negative charge and negligible mass.

They should be able to spot that Student B's response is better because they mention the charges of the particles and their mass, and they have included the fact that different shells contain different numbers of electrons.

Comparative modelling is essential for encouraging students to critique models with precision, so they can then use the models to shape their own work.

4. Share your thinking

This links to live modelling and is popularly referred to as developing metacognition – that is, thinking about thinking. Alongside questions in science, students will often be given some information (e.g. a diagram, graph, table of results, paragraph of writing) that they will be expected to use in their answer. All too often, what we do as science teachers is go straight to the answer section and talk the students through this, without discussing the 'pre-question information' with them. We need to model to our students how we think about this information and then use it to answer the question.

The best way to do this is to project the question onto the whiteboard and then annotate it with your thoughts, discussing your annotations with the students as you go. For example:

- If the information is in text form, highlight some of the key words and scientific ideas in the text and note down their meanings. You could also identify and underline the command words such as 'describe' and 'explain' and discuss what these mean with the students.
- If the information is a graph, highlight and interpret the trends in the graph, with possible explanations.
- If the information is a diagram or flow chart, mark it up with a description of what is happening at each stage/part of the diagram.
- Highlight the number of marks for the question and annotate accordingly (e.g. "Three marks so I need to make three points").

Effectively what you are doing is putting your thinking into words and modelling to the students your thought processes when approaching this particular question. My colleague, geography teacher Ben Crockett, has developed this idea further. Once he has been through this process with his students, he gives them an exam question along with a piece of tracing paper. They place the tracing paper over the exam question and annotate it with their thinking. They can then share their thoughts with others by placing each other's tracing paper onto their question to see their thinking. They then remove the tracing paper to reveal the clean question which they go on to complete.

5. Unpick the method

Science teachers need to regularly model how to do experiments. We diligently show students step by step what to do and how to do it, but we often forget a key part of this modelling process – why we are doing it like that. This is essential in terms of developing students' scientific understanding, but also for ensuring that they are working safely.

While we are modelling practical work to the students, we should remember to punctuate this with questions about why we are doing each step. For example:

- When we are using the measuring cylinder, why should we ensure that our eyes are at the same level as the cylinder?
- Why should we stir the water before we measure the temperature?
- Why do we need to repeat the experiment three times when measuring the time it takes for a marble to fall through different liquids?

As well as embedding good scientific practice, this is also an opportunity to develop and extend their thinking. For example:

- What are the possible sources of human error in this experiment?
- What would be an alternative method to measure the rate of this chemical reaction?

6. Say it back to me

Having shown students how to do a piece of practical work and unpicked it with them, we should check that they really understand how to do it before we let them loose on the equipment. This will avoid confusion and uncertainty when they are doing the practical work themselves, as well as reassuring you that they will be carrying out the work safely. A simple way to do this is to ask the students, one at a time, to repeat the practical procedure back to you and the group. Combine this with Doug Lemov's strategy of cold calling[2] (i.e. directing your questioning at specific students, rather than asking them to offer a response), and remember to keep all the students alert by putting the name of the student you

2 Doug Lemov, *Teach Like a Champion: 49 Techniques that Put Students on the Path to College* [Kindle edn] (San Francisco, CA: Jossey-Bass, 2010).

are directing the question towards at the end of the question. For example:

So what's the first thing you are going to do when you get back to your places ... John?

Thanks, John. What's the next step ... Sarah?

Thanks, Sarah. Why do we need to do that ... Myra?

---

7. Find your own faults

As well as modelling to students how to do the practical work, we should also show them how to find faults with the equipment they are using and how to fix them. This will save you a huge amount of time during practical lessons as it will avoid you having to move from group to group showing them how to solve the same problem. For example, when you are introducing electrical circuits for the first time, model to the students what to do if they set up their circuit and the light bulb isn't working (e.g. try replacing the bulb, the power supply or the leads – in sequence). Similarly, when they use microscopes for the first time, show them how to find their sample and then focus in carefully by starting with the low objective lens and moving up.

You could link this with the idea of comparative modelling. Set up two similar electrical circuits, but have some intentional faults in one (e.g. a voltmeter in series rather than in parallel) and ask the students to identify what is wrong with one of the circuits.

8. Expert examples and scaffolds

As science graduates, we will have seen and read a number of scientific papers and experiment reports. Secondary school students won't be familiar with this genre of expert writing. Therefore, it is worthwhile sharing some examples of experiment reports written by scientists with the students to familiarise them with the style they are aiming for. An Internet search should provide you with a number of examples.

As well as just showing the students these academic papers, pick out some of the key features with them. For example:

- Can we tell what the purpose of the experiment is from the title? How does it achieve this?
- What features of the method would make it easy to follow?
- What have they included in their results table?
- What are the key sections of their conclusion?

This can be developed further by providing the students with scaffolds to help them become scientific writers. Sentence starters work well for this, especially when it comes to practical work. For example:

Introduction

- The purpose of this experiment is to find out …
- I will do this by …
- I expect …
- This is because …
- If this is the case, my results will show that …

Method

- The apparatus I will use will be …
- I have chosen these because …
- My independent variable will be …

- The range will be …
- My controlled variables will be …
- These need to be controlled because …
- My dependent variable will be …
- I will measure this by …
- My step-by-step instructions will be …
- I will ensure accuracy by …
- I will ensure precision by …

Conclusion and evaluation

- The data/graph shows that …
- This can be demonstrated by the following sets of data …
- So the overall trend is …
- This happened because …
- My prediction was … So this data …
- There were/were not any anomalies in my results. I know this because …
- This was because …
- If I were to do the experiment again, I would improve it by …
- This would ensure that …

However, care needs to be taken with sentence starters being used in this way. You should ask yourself:

- How will I ensure that the scaffold offers the opportunity to extend thinking and is not too restrictive?
- Is my scaffold still requiring students to think?
- How will I ensure that scaffolded resources are simple to use and understand, so that they do not inadvertently create an impediment to learning?

- How will I know that the fine balance between support and challenge has been struck?
- When should the scaffolds be removed (because ultimately that is what we are aiming for)?

9. Worked examples

Using scientific formulae to carry out calculations is a key part of the science curriculum. The first time students use a new formula and/or do a calculation go through it one step at a time with them and get them to copy it into their books as you go, discussing the process and questioning them at each stage. When the students have a worked example in their books they can refer back to it when tackling future problems. As they become more confident with the approach they will become less dependent on the worked example, but at this novice stage it will serve as a good model.

Reflective Questions

- Are you confident enough to model on the whiteboard 'live', or are you overly reliant on prepared slides of a piece of science writing or a solution to a scientific calculation?
- Do you show students exemplary pieces of scientific work and then critique them together?
- When you are modelling a response to a question, do you also model your thought processes as you go?
- Do you scaffold your modelling and question the students at each stage to support their learning?
- Do you explain each step of the method carefully as you are modelling how to do practical work?

Chapter 4
Practice

Having explained scientific ideas to students, and then modelled how to use this knowledge, we then need to provide them with the opportunity to practise this for themselves. The purpose of this practice is to use the key knowledge and skills so that it then becomes embedded – that is, they have learnt it. David Didau offers a sensible explanation for learning:

> *To know whether something has been learned we should ask ourselves three questions:*
>
> 1. *Will students still know this next week, next month, next year?*
> 2. *Will students be able to apply what they have been learning in a new example, a new subject, a new place?*
> 3. *How will this transform students' understanding of the world?*[1]

It's clear to see how practice is an essential part of the learning process. However, it's not quite as straightforward as

1 David Didau, A Definition of Learning, *The Learning Spy* (28 January 2016). Available at: http://www.learningspy.co.uk/learning/a-definition-of-learning/.

doing something over and over again. We need to consider the following aspects:

- **Practice doesn't make perfect, it makes permanent.** Simply practising something again and again will not necessarily make students good at something, it will just make it stick. For example, students could be answering lots of questions around balancing chemical equations; however, if they are doing it wrong they will just get better at doing it badly.
- **Repetition is key.** In order to memorise something, we need to come back to it time and time again and practise retrieving it from our memory. The process of retrieval practice helps to strengthen our memory. This is problematic for a subject like science which is very content heavy.
- **Interleaving and spacing.** Cognitive science suggests that to optimise learning we should switch between topics while we are studying them and make links between them.[2] Alongside this, we should space out topics – that is, do a topic, then leave some forgetting time and return to it a few weeks later.
- **Is the practice working?** This is where we often go wrong as science teachers. We tend to teach students a topic in a lesson – for example, the enzymes used in the digestive system. At the end of the lesson we then ask them to recall the names of the enzymes, where they are produced and the substrate on which they work. Unsurprisingly, most students will be able to tell you this, but it does not mean that they have learnt it. If we go back to David Didau's definition of learning, we could only know if they had learnt it (i.e. the practice has been successful) if we tested them on it a week or a month later. We don't often do this.

---

2 Peter C. Brown, Henry L. Roediger III and Mark A. McDaniel, *Make It Stick: The Science of Successful Learning* (Cambridge, MA: Harvard University Press, 2014).

- **Practice should keep them in the struggle zone.** The importance of the struggle zone was discussed in Chapter 1. If practice is going to be productive, we need to ensure that students are working in the struggle zone.

Practice Strategies

1. Low stakes tests

The process of thinking about something helps us to remember it. Daniel Willingham summarises this well: "Memory is the residue of thought."[3]

Cognitive scientists refer to this as retrieval practice – finding opportunities for students to think about topics, with a view to retrieving them from their memory. This is not easy for science teachers as we normally have a very packed curriculum to get through. We need to think about how we can do this in a sustainable way, and low stakes tests are key to this.

Very simply, start every lesson with a nine question, low stakes test. This should comprise three questions on the last lesson, three questions on what they did last week and three questions on what they did last month. Go through the

3 Willingham, *Why Don't Students Like School?*, p. 54.

answers and ask the students to mark them, but don't worry about collecting in the scores. They don't really matter. What matters is the process of thinking about the questions and retrieving the answers from memory.

This principle of retrieval practice can also be applied to homework. Don't just set them questions on what they have done that week; include questions on topics they did last month or last term.

2. Straddling

As a science teacher, it's not always easy to put into practice what we know to be important in terms of effective learning. We know the importance of repetition and retrieval practice, but with a content-heavy subject and limited curriculum time it can be difficult to put this into action. Many schools don't tend to provide opportunities for this, and we move from one topic to another and another in a bid to cover the curriculum:

Topic 1	Topic 2	Topic 3	Topic 4	Topic 5	Topic 6
Lesson 1	Lesson 2	Lesson 3	Lesson 4	Lesson 5	Lesson 6

This limits the opportunity for repetition and retrieval. The notion of having to squeeze things into a single lesson to facilitate effective learning is a false one, but one that has been promoted widely. If we compare this to subjects such as English and maths, this would not be the type of approach used. With these subjects, having embedded essential knowledge (e.g. factorising quadratic equations) and having modelled this with them, the students would then spend a number of lessons practising and embedding this learning – that is, the learning is straddled over a number of lessons. This approach does lend itself to repetition and retrieval.

With just a small shift, science teachers could break away from the topic-by-topic structure and adopt an approach that looks more like this:

Topic 1	Topic 2	Topic 3	Topic 4	Topic 5	Topic 6

Lesson 1	Lesson 2	Lesson 3	Lesson 4	Lesson 5	Lesson 6

For example, topic 1 may have been looking at forces and resultant forces, but to embed this it is carried it on into lesson 2. As it is a fundamental idea, you will want to ensure the students are confident with it before moving on. This would then progress to looking at terminal velocity. The students might pick this up with greater confidence than usual, because you had spent longer embedding the surface knowledge of resultant forces. This is straddled across two lessons before moving on to Hooke's law. This involves a practical which could be carried out in one lesson and then analysed in the next.

This idea of straddling topics across lessons is useful as it stops students from compartmentalising their learning and encourages them to make links between topics. It might take slightly longer to cover the content with this approach but it's time well spent, for the following reasons:

- **Retrieval.** If you are continuing the same topic across lessons, the students have to retrieve knowledge from last lesson to support what they are moving on to.
- **Interleaving.** You are not limiting topics to individual lessons. They are being stretched over a number of lessons and so key ideas are being repeated.

- **Makes links explicit.** As 'topic transitions' are happening during a lesson, it enables you to draw out the connections and common ideas between them, which then become more obvious for the students.
- **Stops artificial 'moving on'.** We tend to assume that the end-of-lesson bell means they have 'got it', and so next lesson we move on to the next topic regardless of whether they have grasped the idea or not. This is often linked to a plenary – probably one of the most poorly practised parts of many lessons. The teacher will often, at best, ask a few students what they have remembered from the last hour or, at worst, tell students what they should have learnt. This will then be used by the teacher as a green light that the class have learnt that topic and that it is okay to move on. The reality, of course, is that this is no way to effectively check learning because learning takes place over time and is a long-term venture. Straddling removes this artificial signal to move on and encourages us to only do so once the students are confident with the topic being taught.

Clearly, straddling has implications for planning. It's easy to plan in terms of "I have X number of topics to fit into Y number of lessons," and so allocate a single topic to each lesson, but is this really supporting learning (i.e. providing opportunities for students to revisit topics)? Hence, planning is a key consideration.

3. Make the links explicit

We need to find opportunities to revisit topics and make it explicit to the students when we are doing so. For example, when we are covering static electricity, this is a perfect opportunity to recap atomic structure. Similarly, when we are teaching the carbon cycle, this is an opportunity to link to processes such as respiration and photosynthesis.

The key is to make it clear to the students that you are linking back to content that has been covered previously. You could, for example, signpost this on your PowerPoint with a symbol that shows you are making links (e.g. a chain) and then ask the students to think about other topics and find connections.

A great time to do this is at the end of the lesson. Rather than taking the traditional plenary approach of, "What have we learnt this lesson?", ask students, "What work have we done in previous lessons that links to what we have covered today?"

4. Exam questions

In the Introduction I mentioned the inspirational science teacher Pam McCulloch. Here, Pam describes how she used exam questions with her students:

Practice is key. We would do lots and lots of exam questions. So when they then came to their actual exams, it was a piece of cake! When doing exam questions we would – recap the knowledge; do the question; go through the answers – focusing on the key terminology and how the answer needs to be constructed. If they didn't get it, I would tell them "Don't worry, you will". But don't let them stay stuck for too long. Work through it with them to show them how, then let them do another one on their own. They love it when they see that they can actually do it. Always make sure they do their corrections – insist on it. Getting it wrong is fine, but they need to learn how to get it right![4]

When science teachers aren't confident about the subject matter they are teaching they often fall into the trap of

4 Shaun Allison, Teaching with Pam, *Class Teaching* (6 April 2014). Available at: https://classteaching.wordpress.com/2014/04/06/teaching-with-pam/.

going through one difficult exam question with a solution that they have already prepared on a PowerPoint slide. This is unfortunate because it doesn't give the students an opportunity to practise lots of difficult questions. The best science teachers will have the confidence to go through and practise plenty of difficult questions with their students. Make it your business to practise some really challenging questions yourself, so when it comes to the lesson you are confident enough to do so with the students.

5. Scanning for perfection

It's important that students know what excellence looks like if they are to engage in 'perfect practice', otherwise they will simply continue to practise getting it wrong. When students are doing a piece of scientific writing, such as describing and explaining a set of experimental results, move around the room looking for a 'perfect answer'. Once you have found one, read it out to the class or show it to them using a visualiser. You can then spend time as a class discussing what made it so good and what they need to do to get their work up to that standard. This should then inform their practice moving forward. You can then continue to scan the students as they are working, making sure that the individuals who should be updating their work actually are.

6. Spacing

Cognitive science suggests that if we are taught a topic, then are allowed to forget it before coming back to it weeks or months later and having to retrieve it from our memory, our memory of that topic is strengthened.[5] This is difficult in a topic like science where we are under pressure to work through a huge amount of curricular content. However, there are some simple ways in which we can address this:

- Once a month, schedule in a 'spacing lesson'. During this lesson, break from the topic you are currently teaching and give the students some questions on a topic they covered two or three weeks ago. If you feel unable to dedicate a whole lesson to this, maybe just do it for the first twenty minutes.
- Spaced homework questions. As we saw in the section on low stakes tests, you can set homework tasks that include some questions that link back to work they did a week, a month or a term ago.

7. Knowledge organisers

English teacher Joe Kirby has written very eloquently about the use of 'knowledge organisers'.[6] A knowledge organiser is simply a table that contains the key knowledge that

5 John Dunlosky, Katherine A. Rawson, Elizabeth J. Marsh, Mitchell J. Nathan and Daniel T. Willingham, Improving Students' Learning with Effective Learning Techniques: Promising Directions from Cognitive and Educational Psychology, *Psychological Science in the Public Interest* 14(1) (2013): 4–58.

6 Joe Kirby, Knowledge Organisers, *Pragmatic Education* (28 March 2015). Available at: https://pragmaticreform.wordpress.com/2015/03/28/knowledge-organisers/.

students need to remember. Here is an extract from a chemistry example:

Science knowledge organiser – C1

Fundamental ideas	
Atom	Simplest particle that substances are made from – contains protons, neutrons and electrons.
Element	A substance made of only one type of atom.
Proton	Positively charged particle in the nucleus of an atom.
Neutron	Neutrally charged particle in the nucleus of an atom.
Electron	Negatively charged particle that orbits the nucleus.
Atomic number	The number of protons an element has. All atoms of the same element have the same number of protons.
Mass number	The sum of the protons and neutrons in an atom.
Shells	Electron shells hold electrons. The first shell (nearest the nucleus) holds 2, subsequent shells hold up to 8.
Group	Columns in the periodic table. Elements in the same group have the same number of electrons in their outer shell (energy level).

Fundamental ideas	
Noble gases	Group 0 in the periodic table. They are unreactive because their outer shells are full.
Ion	An atom that has gained or lost electrons. Those that gain electrons become negative ions and those that lose electrons become positive ions.
Compound	When atoms join together during a chemical reaction, they form a compound.
Reactants	The substances that react together in a chemical reaction.
Products	The substances that are produced during a chemical reaction.

Limestone and building materials	
Limestone	Mainly composed of calcium carbonate and is a building material.
Thermal decomposition	Using heat to break down molecules such as calcium carbonate.
Calcium oxide	Produced by the thermal decomposition of calcium carbonate.
Calcium hydroxide	An alkali that is produced by adding water to calcium oxide.

Limestone and building materials	
Limewater	A solution of calcium hydroxide that turns cloudy in the presence of carbon dioxide (because it produces calcium carbonate).
Cement	Produced when limestone is heated with clay.
Mortar	Cement and sand added together (with water).
Concrete	Cement, sand and aggregate added together (with water).

Metals and their uses	
Ore	A compound of a metal and other elements (e.g. iron oxide).
Reduction	The removal of oxygen from a substance (e.g. iron oxide is reduced by carbon to make iron).
Blast furnace	Where iron oxide is reduced using carbon on an industrial scale.
Electrolysis	A method of extracting metals that are more reactive than carbon from their ores – by using electricity.
Smelting	A method of extracting metals like copper from ores by heating them in a furnace.

Knowledge organisers are used in a similar way to how we learnt to spell: we would learn the words, cover them up, write them out and then check our spellings. This process was then repeated and, of course, it worked. They are a great tool for helping students to remember core knowledge and support the idea of retrieval practice.

Students can be asked to learn a section of the knowledge organiser at a time (e.g. the 'fundamental ideas' section), either for homework or at the start of the lesson. You can then project the key words onto the whiteboard and ask the students to recall and write down the correct definition. They then self-check and mark their work. How they do this self-checking can be developed in a number of ways:

- They can award themselves a full mark if they get the definition exactly right or half a mark if it was nearly there.
- If they get the definition wrong they can rewrite the correct definition underneath.
- They can put a star by the ones they couldn't remember as a reminder to re-learn that word later.

The use of knowledge organisers can then be extended further, in lessons or at home:

- Parents can use them at home to test students on key terminology.
- Students can use them to create sets of flashcards to use at home – either on card or on an app on their smartphone.
- Students could be asked to use each of the key words in a sentence to demonstrate that they fully understand the meaning of the word.
- Students could use the knowledge organiser as a checklist as they work through the topic (if they are given it when they first start the topic).

- Over time the organisers build up into a great record of the ideas students have struggled with, which can then serve to focus their revision later.

8. Comprehension exercises

Getting students to read a passage of scientific writing and then answer some skilfully crafted questions on it is a valuable exercise. Not only does it expose the students to challenging scientific texts, but it also requires them to use their existing knowledge, develops their ideas further and encourages them to see the links between different areas.

Here are some points to consider when designing comprehension exercises:

- Choose a text that will challenge the students. It should contain some of the core knowledge that they need for reinforcement, but should also extend and develop these ideas. Scientific journals and websites are a good source.
- Begin with some questions that will simply pick out the key knowledge (e.g. "The article talks about extracting DNA from the cell. Which part of the cell contains the DNA?").
- Encourage the students to discuss the questions and, in particular, what knowledge they need to use in order to answer them.
- Include questions that will require the students to think more deeply about the content. These questions should get them to think about the topic beyond what is mentioned in the article and link other scientific ideas together.
- Finish by asking them to write a summary of the article in three bullet points.

9. Say it … spell it

This technique encourages the repetition of key ideas and encourages the students to practise saying complex scientific words out loud – almost like a chant! For example:

Teacher: What is the tissue that lines the trachea called?

A student (who you have asked to respond)*: Ciliated epithelial.*

Teacher: Now everybody say it.

Students: Ciliated epithelial.

Teacher: And again.

(Repeat a number of times.)

Teacher: Now spell it.

You can vary your approach here: ask one student to spell it, or the class to say one letter at a time, or one student to say three letters, then another student says three letters and so on.

Teacher: Now tell me what the tissue looks like.

(Repeat a number of times with different students.)

---

10. Overlearn

Cognitive science suggests that once we have learnt something to the point of mastery – that is, being able to recall or do something with confidence – we shouldn't then leave it. We should continue to practise it so that it becomes automatic. This is the idea of overlearning.[7] The best netball players won't stop practising shooting once they have mastered it. They will practise and practise so that when they get into a shooting position in a match they will shoot automatically. While this is fine in theory, it is not so easy for the busy science teacher who has a great deal of content to get through. How can science teachers address this?

- Take every opportunity to overlearn the 'big ideas' mentioned in Chapter 2 (e.g. the parts of a cell or subatomic particles). For example, start lessons with a quick verbal test of this core knowledge.
- Use homework to overlearn topics that have been covered in lessons.
- Give students lots of opportunities to complete exam questions on the topic, not just in the lesson in which they have learnt the content, but in future lessons when they have moved on to a different topic.

---

7 Daniel T. Willingham, What Will Improve a Student's Memory? *American Educator* (winter 2008–2009): 17–25. Available at: http://www.aft.org/sites/default/files/periodicals/willingham_0.pdf.

Reflective Questions

- Do you monitor the practice that students are doing, so they are not simply embedding bad habits?
- Do you find opportunities to repeat key learning points during the lesson?
- Do you find opportunities to review topics that were taught a lesson ago, a week ago or a month ago?
- Do you use low stakes quizzes regularly at the start of lessons?
- Does the practice that your students do keep them in the struggle zone?
- Do you make the links between the topics you have taught explicit to the students?
- Do you provide the students with the opportunity to practise lots of exam questions?

Chapter 5

Questioning

As science teachers we should stop and think about why we ask our students questions. We do so for a variety of reasons:

- To test understanding of a new scientific concept. We can explain a scientific idea, model how to use it and then provide students with the time to practise using this new knowledge and skill. However, to really test their understanding we need to ask them questions about it.
- To deepen and develop their understanding of scientific concepts. In order to challenge students, and to make them think with depth and breadth, we need to ask them probing questions.
- To ensure that students take a share in the cognitive work of the lesson. It's important that all students make a contribution to the thinking that is taking place during a lesson. Involving as many students as possible in this can be facilitated through questioning.
- To help you form and sustain an academic culture in your science laboratory. This is so important for setting the right tone in your lessons. By questioning students and making them think deeply through your questions, you are nurturing a knowledge-rich classroom.

- To encourage students to retrieve things from memory in order to strengthen it.
- To create curiosity – a key attribute for all scientists!

We should also consider what makes a good question. Dylan Wiliam and Paul Black suggest the following:[1]

- One which promotes discussion.
- One which everyone can make a stab at.
- One which makes pupils think.
- One which has a specific purpose.

While it is clear that questioning is pivotal to great science teaching, it is worth exploring the mistakes that teachers often make with questioning:

- Our wait time for students to respond to a question is too short, often less than a second. This doesn't really give the students enough time to think about and formulate a response.
- We can sometimes respond weakly to students' answers. Our own subject knowledge needs to be strong if we are going to engage with the multitude of responses that the students could give and avoid embedding misconceptions.
- Giving a detailed expert commentary in response to each answer, which can sometimes serve to confuse students if it is not unpicked with them.
- Questioning can sometimes involve only a few students – usually the ones we know are going to give a good answer!
- We are frequently overly accepting of poor answers, due to time pressures or a misguided view that it will make the students feel better about themselves.
- Asking ineffective questions that provide very little challenge and often simply require mimicry from students

1 Dylan Wiliam and Paul Black, *Inside the Black Box: Raising Standards Through Classroom Assessment* (London: GL Assessment, 1990).

(i.e. the teacher tells the students something and then five minutes later asks them a question about it). Unsurprisingly, most students will be able to recall the answer, but they will be unlikely to do so in a month or more.

- When a student says "I don't know", simply moving the question on to another student, without scaffolding your questioning and building their response.
- Ping-pong between the teacher and one student – this can get quite tedious for the rest of the class.
- We sometimes question students when they don't really have the knowledge to answer the question because they haven't been taught it yet. When this is the case, we simply need to explain the new knowledge to them.

Questioning Strategies

1. Dialogic questioning

Dialogic questioning is what the best science teachers do so effortlessly but so effectively. Having asked an initial question, they will then ask a range of follow-up questions based on student responses to probe and deepen their thinking. When this is being done well it seems like a conversation is happening around the room that is delving deeper and deeper into the topic. In order to do this, of course, you need to have excellent subject knowledge and be able to think on your feet. You also need to know where you want the students to get to in their thinking and how your questioning will direct them to that point.

Teacher: What's the purpose of respiration?

Student: To provide us with energy.

Teacher: Yes. Is it a chemical reaction?

Student: Yes.

Teacher: Why?

Student: Because two things react and make something else.

Teacher: What two things react?

Student: Sugar and oxygen.

Teacher: Sugar? Can we be more precise?

Student: Glucose and oxygen.

Teacher: What are the products?

(No response)

Teacher: What do I mean by products?

Student: The substances that are made in a chemical reaction.

Teacher: Great. So what are they in respiration?

Student: Carbon dioxide and water.

Teacher: So where does the glucose and oxygen come from?

And on it goes. Through relentless and focused questioning, the teacher is teasing out the key learning points. When doing this you can often cover a large amount of knowledge, so it's worth using the students' responses to shape some notes, a diagram or a flowchart on the board as you go.

2. Delayed response

Often, rather than just wanting to find out if a student knows something, where a quick question will suffice, we want to know how deeply the students understand something. To do this we should give them sufficient time to think about and formulate their responses. A good way to do this is to tell students in advance that you are going to ask them a question, explain what the question is and how long they have got to think about it. For example, the students might be doing a written piece of work where they need to evaluate the advantages and disadvantages of limestone quarrying. When they are about halfway through the task, stop them and say something like, "In four minutes' time, I'm going to stop you and ask you to give me either one advantage or one disadvantage of limestone quarrying." This takes away some of the anxiety of answering questions as it gives them time to consider their response.

Similarly, when it comes to practical work, tell the students at the start of the practical the key question that you will be asking them when they have finished. For example, they may have been carrying out an experiment to look at the effect of temperature on the rate of a chemical reaction. Tell them before they start, "At the end of the practical I will be asking you to suggest some possible sources of error and inaccuracy with this method." This will encourage the students to give this some thought during the practical work.

3. Cold calling

This is a fantastic strategy from Doug Lemov.[2] Often when we are asking students questions, it will go something like this: "Sarah, can you tell me what the function of the nucleus of the cell is please?" As soon as you say "Sarah" the rest of the class can sit back, safe in the knowledge that they are not going to be asked to answer the question. Much better to reshape the question and rephrase it like this: "What is the function of the nucleus of the cell … (pause) … Sarah?"

The question has been asked but anyone could be asked to answer it. Therefore, all students need to be thinking about a possible response because, following the pause, they could be the one asked. From one question you are generating thinking across the whole classroom. Like all of the most effective teaching strategies, cold calling requires very little planning by the teacher but it has great impact.

4. Deep questioning

To encourage students to think more deeply we should ask them questions that encourage them to reflect on their own thinking. For example:

- Why do you think that is the case?
- How did you come up with that response?

---

2 Lemov, *Teach Like a Champion.*

- How could you add more detail to that response?
- What was the hardest thing about answering that question?
- Lots of people respond to that question by saying X. Why didn't you?
- What might be an alternative view to your response?
- How does that link to what we were talking about last lesson?
- What theory would you use to explain the results you obtained from that practical?
- Are the results from your practical as you expected? Why?

It is really important that everybody listens to this exchange and that you encourage them to do so by bringing others into the questioning: "Evie, what do you think of the answer that Josh just gave? Do you agree with it? Why?"

By encouraging students to articulate their thoughts and think in a metacognitive way we are supporting them in selecting the best cognitive tools for the problem they are trying to solve. This is useful for the individual student, as we are validating their reasoning and so encouraging them to do more of it. However, it is also important for the other students, as they are having useful cognitive processes modelled for them. This can only be a good thing.

5. The big question

At the start of the lesson, write a really hard question on the board that the students won't necessarily know the answer to at the outset but should be able to answer by the end of the lesson (e.g. Can you describe the process of genetic engineering in detail?), or link this to a practical they will be doing (e.g. How will temperature affect the action of the enzyme amylase on starch?).

Bring this to the attention of students early on and tell them that they will be asked to answer the question at the end of the lesson. Keep referring to the question throughout and reminding them that they will be asked to answer it presently. This also helps to give a context and a purpose to any practical work they are doing.

The big question is a useful replacement for the more sterile 'learning objective' that won't really mean a great deal to the students. A hard question that seems insurmountable at the start of the lesson, but becomes increasingly accessible as the lesson progresses, has far more purpose.

6. Hinge questions

In science, it is important that students have a strong grasp of the surface learning before we move them on to the deep learning. Hinge questions are a great way of doing this. A hinge question is a very targeted question, used at a strategic point in the lesson; when you want to check the understanding of all the students before moving the learning on.

A good hinge question should be:

- Quick and easy for the teacher to ask.
- Quick for the students to respond to – it is for this reason that multiple-choice questions are a popular option.

- Devised so that a student will only get the answer right if they understand the key point.
- Designed so that wrong responses inform the teacher about any misconceptions the students may have.

For example, the students might be asked this hinge question about osmosis:

What is the correct definition of osmosis?

a. *The process by which molecules of water tend to pass through a semi-permeable membrane from a less concentrated solution into a more concentrated one.*

b. *The process by which substances move from a high concentration to a low concentration.*

c. *The process by which molecules of water tend to pass through a semi-permeable membrane from a solution with a high concentration into a more diluted solution.*

d. *The process by which molecules of water tend to pass from a less concentrated solution into a more concentrated one.*

The correct answer is of course (a). If students pick (b) they haven't understood that osmosis is a very specific form of diffusion – the diffusion of water molecules. If they pick (c) they are confused about the terminology used to describe solutions, confusing a high concentration of water molecules (a diluted solution) with a concentrated solution. Finally, if they pick (d) they haven't grasped the important point that osmosis takes place across a semi-permeable membrane. It's clear to see how hinge questions can be used as a great diagnostic tool for science teachers.

One of the perceived purposes of questioning in the classroom is to elicit student understanding on a topic, and hinge questions are great for doing this. In reality, though, it is hard to carry out effectively in order to get meaningful feedback about student understanding with around thirty students in a classroom. It is just not feasible to get a proper verbal response to each question from all of the students – it would just take too long. Mini whiteboards provide a solution to this problem, as they allow the teacher to ask a question that all the students can respond to. The teacher can then scan all the responses and make a judgement about how well the students have understood that particular idea. (Mini whiteboards are discussed in more detail in Chapter 6.)

7. Redirect

An essential skill of a great science teacher is redirecting incorrect student responses so they eventually get to the right answer. For example, the question might be, "What happens to the thermal energy from a light bulb?" The student may respond by saying, "It is lost." At this point you want to question them further, to redirect them away from the misconception that energy is lost and towards the fact that it is transferred and dissipates. A redirecting question could be, "Is it really lost? Is it no longer there?" They may say yes to this so more redirection is required: "So if you put your hand close to the light bulb, how would the air feel?" Hopefully they will respond to this by saying that it feels warm. By continuing along this line you can eventually get them to the point where they understand that the energy hasn't been lost but in fact has been transferred to the air.

Be careful here though. It's important that redirecting uses questioning to scaffold the students' thinking towards the correct answer. It is not about simply telling them the answer or making the question so pointed that it's virtually impossible to get it wrong.

8. Open and closed questions

In recent years, it has become unfashionable to promote closed questions (i.e. a question where there is a right or wrong answer). The trend has been to encourage the use of open questions (i.e. questions that elicit an extended answer with a number of possible options). In science, both are useful and we should not shy away from using either. For example, sometimes we just need to know if the students know certain things (e.g. the number of protons in a carbon atom, the parts of a cell, the components of an electrical circuit diagram). This is how we test their surface learning and the best way to do this is by using closed questions.

Alongside this, we also need to probe them further and will often follow this up with a more open question: "It's great that you know the function of the mitochondria and ribosomes. Can you explain how they work together?" This question will require a more extended response.

Both open and closed questions are valuable and both serve an important purpose.

9. Teacher listening

An essential part of asking good questions as a teacher is being a good listener. This allows us to formulate effective questions that will prompt thinking and clarity of understanding. Here are some points to consider:

- Listen to the content of student ideas in their response to you. This allows you to direct your questioning around accuracy and misconceptions. For example, a student might say, "The voltage of the battery is …" Your questioning should guide them to rephrase this and talk about the potential difference of a battery.
- Listening for the form of ideas being expressed gives you a feel for how well a student's knowledge and understanding is structured. Is it clear or are there gaps in their explanation? Is this typical of the student and the class? If so, it would be useful to frame your questioning around these gaps.
- When a student responds to a question, consider how the response came about. Did they struggle to come up with the answer? Was it intuitive or was it worked out? You might then want to question them further about how they worked it out, as this will encourage other students to reflect on their own thinking process.

10. Managing student discussions

As science teachers, we often need to support student discussions around a range of topics, including ethical issues (e.g. Is adult cell cloning ethical? Do you agree that limestone quarrying should be expanded? Should we be building more nuclear power stations?).

Managing student discussions effectively is essential for a number of reasons:

- It creates structured dialogue that builds synergy between talking and writing.
- Discussion helps students to realise that the truth is inherently slippery.

- It helps students to structure their thoughts and arguments.
- It helps the teacher to create structured and disciplined discussions.
- Probing questioning develops verbal reasoning skills.
- There is no 'get out' clause – students are compelled to participate.
- It challenges teachers to develop our own questioning skills.

In his blog, Andy Tharby talks about a strategy he uses in his English lessons that can be transferred to science. He calls it 'probing the continuum'.[3] Start by drawing a large line on your board, alongside the question to be discussed. For example:

Should we use adult cell cloning to improve cattle disease resistance?

Yes ⟷ **No**

Instructions for discussion	**Knowledge prompts**
Agree with **B**uild upon **C**hallenge Hand up – to make a point Three fingers up – comment on another's viewpoint Fist up – ask a question	Sperm Egg Nucleus Zygote Fertilisation Cell Embryo Body cell

3 Andy Tharby, Probing the Continuum, *Reflecting English* (16 January 2014). Available at: https://reflectingenglish.wordpress.com/2014/01/16/simply-the-best-post-it-note-discussion-rocks/.

Students are asked to think about this question, come to a decision, put their name on a sticky note and place their note on the continuum arrow based on what they think. Students are also given some instructions in the form of a table. The column on the left tells the students how they should engage with responses from their peers – they should remember to ABC: either agree with, build upon or challenge the response.[4] The column on the right provides them with prompts of the knowledge they should be using when discussing the topic.

Having set the scene, you can then start the discussion by picking a sticky note from the far right of the continuum and asking that person to explain the reasons that led them to this judgement. You can then develop the debate by asking the same question of someone from the far left of the continuum. Immediately you have heard two different viewpoints which can be a stimulus for other people to contribute by sticking up their hand, fist or three fingers.

As the discussion proceeds you should be monitoring who is and who isn't contributing. If you notice one of the group not participating in the discussion, ask them why they placed their sticky note where they did. If their response is "Dunno!" respond with, "That's fine. What I'd like you to do is think about it for a minute, then I'll come back to you and you can tell me your thoughts." Continue asking other people but eventually come back to the reticent student. Having realised they are not going to get away with "dunno" they will probably come up with a great response.

During the discussion, the skill of the teacher – in terms of keeping the discussion going and ensuring wide involvement – is to maintain the right balance between students responding (by hands/fists/three fingers up) and choosing names

---

4 The ABC questioning approach comes from English teacher Alex Quigley's *The Confident Teacher: Developing Successful Habits of Mind, Body and Pedagogy* (Abingdon: Routledge, 2016).

from the sticky notes on the continuum. Your questions will also need to maintain a great level of challenge:

- Why do you think that?
- What do you think of X's response?
- How does that relate to what X has just said?
- Can you develop that answer more by giving some examples?
- Are you still in the middle? Why is that?

There are many ways in which this technique can be developed.

- Praise the students when they use words/terms from the knowledge prompts. This shows they are supporting their point with good knowledge.
- Give students the opportunity to move their sticky notes during the discussion – but they have to explain why.
- Give some students a piece of information (e.g. the viewpoint of a particular stakeholder, such as a farmer or an animal rights activist) and ask them to use this when making their judgement. This is a good way of challenging their views and demonstrating that judgements should be based on evidence.
- It is a great introductory task to a piece of balanced writing – if they can say it, they will find it easier to write it.
- When justifying their viewpoint, encourage the students to make links to other topics that have been studied in other lessons.

Reflective Questions

- Do you ask follow-on questions when students respond to your initial questions to deepen their thinking about the topic?

- When the students don't know the answer to a question, do you scaffold their responses by carefully developing your questions?
- Do you use questions to assess how well the students understand key scientific ideas?
- Do you ensure that your questioning involves as many students as possible?
- Do you give the students sufficient thinking time to consider the responses they are going to make?
- Do you use questioning to carefully move students from surface learning to deep learning?

Chapter 6
Feedback

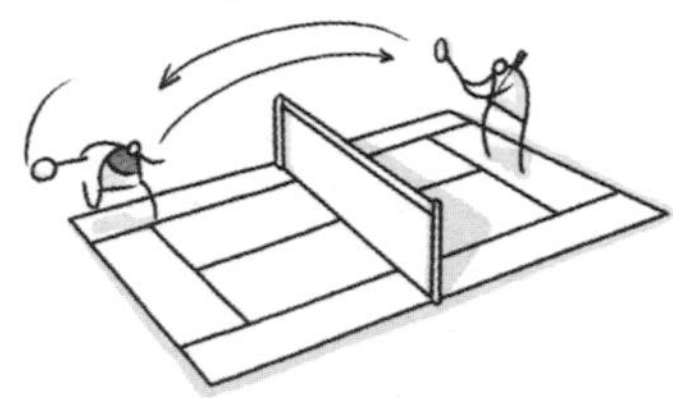

When thinking about feedback, this quote from Dylan Wiliam makes an excellent starting point: "If there's a single principle teachers need to digest about classroom feedback, it's this: The only thing that matters is what students do with it."[1]

Unfortunately, it appears that this is not always the focus for feedback in schools. In a recent report by the Independent Teacher Workload Review Group, the issues around one form of feedback, marking, have been clearly highlighted:

> *Marking has evolved into an unhelpful burden for teachers, when the time it takes is not repaid in positive impact on pupils' progress. This is frequently because it is serving a different purpose such as demonstrating teacher performance or to satisfy the requirements of other, mainly adult, audiences. Too often, it is the marking itself which is being monitored and commented on by leaders rather than pupil outcomes and progress as a result of quality feedback.*[2]

1 Dylan Wiliam, Is the Feedback You're Giving Students Helping or Hindering? *Dylan Wiliam Center* (29 November 2014). Available at: http://www.dylanwiliamcenter.com/is-the-feedback-you-are-giving-students-helping-or-hindering/.

2 Independent Teacher Workload Review Group, *Eliminating Unnecessary Workload Around Marking* (London: Department for Education, 2016). Available at: https://www.gov.uk/government/uploads/system/uploads/attachment_data/file/511256/Eliminating-unnecessary-workload-around-marking.pdf, p. 6.

As science teachers, we should be using a variety of feedback strategies for a number of different purposes. The key reasons we use feedback include:

- To let students know if they are right or wrong. Science is a knowledge-rich subject, so often students simply need to know if they have remembered something or not (e.g. Do they know the function of the cell membrane? Do they know the charges of electrons, protons and neutrons?).
- To encourage students to think more deeply. Once students have mastered the surface learning (e.g. electrons are negatively charged, protons are positive and neutrons are neutral), we should be providing them with feedback through questioning to deepen their thinking (e.g. What would happen to the overall charge if an atom lost an electron?).
- To help students improve the quality of their written work. Whether this is a piece of written work they have done in a lesson or a response to a question in a test, students need to be given feedback about how to improve their work. For example, in a question where they are asked to 'describe and explain' a trend in a set of experimental results, they may well have described the trend but not necessarily have explained it. This is the feedback they will need.
- To help students carry out practical work effectively. When they are conducting practical experiments, we need to be constantly scanning the laboratory to ensure that students are carrying out the experiment both safely and effectively, to enable them to get a secure set of results. If they aren't, they need feedback to help them improve their practical performance.
- To inform your planning. Feedback is very much a two-way process:

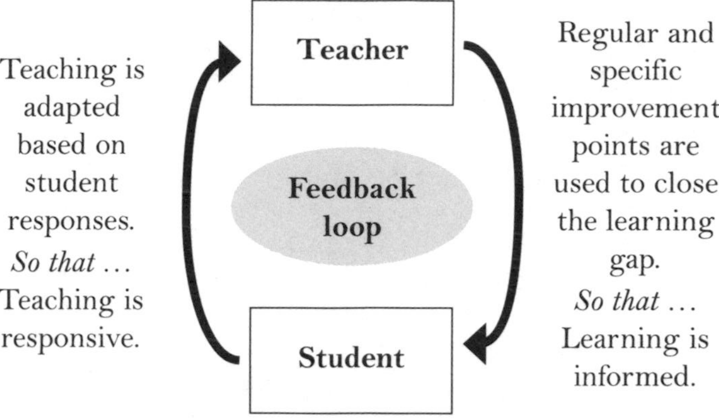

As well as giving feedback to students to help them improve their learning in these ways, feedback is also essential for the teacher. We should use feedback about how students are performing in lessons to inform our future lesson planning. For example, following a lesson on momentum calculations, you may have noticed towards the end of the lesson that the students were not quite getting it. Rather than moving on to the next topic, it's worth investing some time in the next lesson to unpick their mistakes and give them some more time to practise the calculations.

Feedback Strategies

The feedback strategies we use should fit these principles:

- Feedback that simply tells students what to do is unhelpful. This type of feedback compounds dependency.
- Feedback should make students think about their work and how they could develop it. This type of feedback develops autonomy.
- Feedback should make students do something to improve. If it doesn't achieve this, then it is a waste of time.

- Feedback should keep students in the struggle zone. If it just keeps them in the comfort zone, or pushes them into the panic zone, then learning will be limited.
- Feedback should be manageable and sustainable for teachers. This is key for teacher workload and well-being.

1. Self-checking

In science, there are some things that are simply right or wrong (e.g. labelling the organs in the digestive system, physics calculations, the number of electrons in each shell). The most efficient way to give students feedback on this is to go through the answers with them, asking them to check their work as you go. Students should get into the habit of ticking correct answers and correcting their mistakes as you work through the answers. This enables you to do a quick visual scan as you move around the room to see how they have got on. From this you can see if there are any common mistakes that the students have made and reteach that topic if necessary.

You can get more detailed feedback on how the class have done by simply asking the students to give a show of hands for how many out of ten they got correct. This can be developed further by asking for a show of hands for a correct response after each question (but there is no need to record this information). This can be useful as it gives feedback to the teacher on whether there is something that numerous students are struggling to recall or failing to understand. This may highlight the need for instant intervention. If all pupils get a total of nine out of ten then this is obviously great, but if nearly all the students got the same question wrong we can be responsive and act immediately.

This approach gives the students instant feedback on their performance, requires them to address their mistakes, gives useful feedback to teachers about individual and whole-class performance and, most importantly, is manageable and sustainable for teachers.

2. Live marking

Live marking is an effective strategy for science teachers as we want to be able to give students feedback about their understanding of a scientific concept there and then. While students are working, look at their workbooks, picking a piece that is focused on the key learning point for that lesson. Write a question in their book to develop their thinking or correct a misunderstanding, ask them to respond to it and then move away. Come back in a few minutes to check that they have responded. This is a very powerful form of feedback because it's in the context of the work they are doing, it makes them think and it requires them to do something straight away.

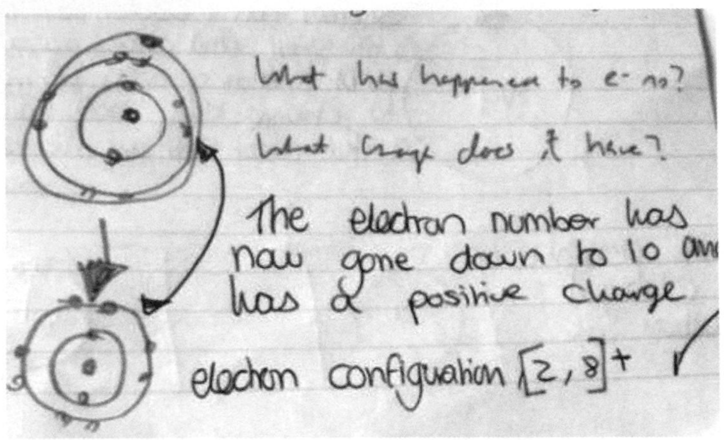

You won't be able to do this with every student in every lesson, but aim to do so with as many as you can. Once you get into the habit of doing it, over the course of a fortnight or so you should be able to cover the majority of students. This has to be more effective and more manageable than taking home sets of books and spending hours writing comments on work that the students did two or three weeks ago, to which they probably won't respond. You can also be targeted with your live marking – for example, by focusing it on specific students who may have been underachieving.

Steph Temple, who teaches science at Durrington High School, uses live marking to prompt student thinking, but also for a variety of other reasons:

As well as using live marking to ask students questions to develop their thinking, I will also use it to underline a mistake, and then ask the student to think about their work – what was the mistake and what do they need to do to get better? I also use it as an opportunity to reinforce my high expectations in terms of presentation – maybe a little unfashionable but very important! It is also useful to 'unstick' students who are struggling to get started. For example, if students are asked to write a paragraph about 'pathogens and body defences', when faced with a blank page they can struggle to get started. However, I will start them off with a sentence starter, e.g. "Pathogens are microorganisms that cause disease. The two main types are …" This can often be enough to get them started. Finally, it's great for embedding the spelling of scientific words. I will underline the word they have spelled incorrectly, tell them the correct spelling and then expect them to write it out again three times.

---

3. Exit tickets

Case study by Damian Benney, deputy head teacher at Penyrheol Comprehensive School, Swansea, Wales

One issue that all science teachers will face is getting through the curriculum in time for the external exams. This is because of the volume of content in the science curriculum. As a consequence it can be too easy to plough through the material and lose sight over whether pupils are understanding the concepts as this content-heavy curriculum is being covered. We need to maximise the opportunities we have to check on the pupils' understanding of the key scientific concepts as we teach them. The feedback it gives us is invaluable. Of course, if a pupil understands something today there is no guarantee that they will remember it in a week or a month's time. But surely we want to make sure that we take the opportunity to check for misconceptions and put them right before that student moves on? Exit tickets, as long as they are well designed, provide this invaluable opportunity for checking for understanding.

The work of Harry Fletcher-Wood has been important in clarifying my thinking in this area.[3] Reading his work has enabled me to design a set of exit tickets to run through the science course. Many teachers will give out sticky notes as

---

3 See https://improvingteaching.co.uk/.

exit tickets and ask pupils to write on them 'three things they have learnt', 'one area they are still struggling with' or 'one thing they would still like to know', and while these are interesting in terms of feedback for the teacher, they have a very limited value in checking for understanding. Exit tickets need to be designed so they can pull apart student understanding and expose misconceptions if they have them. Exit tickets can be given at the end of every lesson, but mine are designed to be given out roughly every few lessons or once a topic has been covered. Good exit tickets will cover the key learning objective of the lesson or the series of lessons.

My exit tickets are usually tweaked versions of previous exam questions. When designing the ticket I have to ensure that the tickets don't just have pupils repeating back parrot fashion what they have covered in the lesson. This will not expose student misunderstanding and can give the impression that all students have understood when this may not be the case. Good exit tickets should show some element of transfer of the scientific knowledge as opposed to regurgitation or mimicry. For example, the exit ticket which followed a few lessons looking at natural selection can be seen on page 105.

During the lessons we hadn't looked at the evolution of the peppered moth. In a previous lesson we had studied the evolution of the coat colour of deer mice from black to brown following the formation of the sand hills where these mice lived. Pupils needed to spot that while the surface details in these two examples are different, they have the same deep structure which is natural selection and a gene mutation which gives offspring an advantageous trait in this changed environment.

The exit tickets should take around five minutes for the pupils to complete. My aim is to skim through them in around the same time and then place each ticket into one of three piles: got it, omissions and misconceptions. What I do

Exit ticket
RAG123

Name:

Kingdom: Animalia

Phylum: Arthropoda

Class: Insecta

Order: Lepidoptera

Family: Geometridae

Genus: Biston

Species: Betularia

What is the scientific name of the peppered moth?

The usual form of the peppered moth is white. In the 1800s, tree bark became black with soot and in the years that followed the population of black moths increased and the white population decreased. Use natural selection to explain how this happened.

....

....

....

....

....

....

....

....

....

....

at the start of the next lesson really depends on the relative size of each pile. If the misconception pile is large then the concept of natural selection will need to be retaught. Of course, this cuts into precious curriculum time, but the alternative is to plough on and not address these misconceptions. Another option is to tailor the opening task of the next lesson to these three piles. Yet another option is to sit all the pupils with misconceptions around one table at the start of the next lesson and reteach this while the rest of the class complete their 'do now' task. However, simply knowing your pupils will give you your direction on what to do next. In general, at the start of the next lesson, sharing some of the better exit tickets via a visualiser will allow those with some omissions to annotate their tickets, and this gives me time to clarify the key concepts with the small number of pupils with misconceptions. This takes a few minutes, and it is a few minutes well spent.

As well as allowing me the invaluable opportunity to be responsive and to feed back to students as part of ongoing quality control, it also gives me feedback on my own teaching and how I can improve it next time I teach that topic. If some pupils are under the impression that the black tree bark *causes* the mutation of the gene, then this is something for me to build into my explanations for the following year. I would now know that the idea that the mutation is random needs further reinforcing the next time I teach it. In terms of feedback, both to the teacher and to the learners, it doesn't get better than a well-designed exit ticket! This is a great example of responsive teaching to immediately close the learning gap.

4. Checklists

Peer and self-assessment can be fraught with danger. Understanding assessment criteria and the specifics about how to improve is difficult for a number of adults, so students will certainly struggle to do it accurately. In fact, there is a real risk that by misinterpreting the criteria, students will give incorrect feedback to either themselves or their peers and embed misconceptions.

Checklists can be used to overcome these issues. As long as they are concise and very specific, they can be given to students while they are tackling a problem to help them ensure they are responding appropriately. This supports them with self-checking their work as they are doing it.

For example, when carrying out physics calculations, students often lose marks because of small mistakes (e.g. not including the formula or the units). Rather than just leaving the students to make these common mistakes, and then having to give them lots of feedback later, why not give them a checklist like the one below which they can use to check their work as they go.

Have you …	**Tick**
Written out the formula you will use?	
Rearranged the formula appropriately?	
Substituted in the numbers from the question?	
Included all the steps in the calculation?	
Written the answer out in full?	
Included the units?	

It's very important that the checklists are composed of clear statements that students can easily interpret and check their work against. They are useful because they instil a sense of confidence in the students by clarifying exactly how to solve a problem or carry out a task which previously may have seemed insurmountable. In fact, it makes them feel like an expert! Like any scaffold, eventually you want to move to a position where the students don't need to use these checklists. However, in the early stages of their practice it's a useful tool to use with students as they move from dependency to independence.

5. Post-assessment DIRT (Dedicated Improvement and Reflection Time)[4]

At some point, most students across all year groups will carry out an assessment in science. This usually comprises exam-style questions that have been put together based on the topic that is currently being studied. From this, the students will probably receive a mark that may have been converted into a percentage score or even a grade. This serves a purpose in terms of telling the students how well they have done relative to their peers, and if they look a bit closer (i.e. where they picked up marks) it should also tell them what they know.

However, the most useful aspect of an assessment like this is often overlooked: it should give students (and teachers) feedback about what they *don't* know, so they can then do something about it. A well-thought-out post-assessment DIRT task along the following lines should facilitate this.

- When marking the assessments, make a note of the common mistakes or targets for improvement, giving each one a T code (T1, T2, etc.). For example, following a Year 7 test on food:
    - T1 – learn food tests
    - T2 – identify food groups
    - T3 – describe food group functions
    - T4 – define the term 'balanced diet'

4 For more on DIRT see Jackie Beere, *The Perfect (Ofsted) Lesson*, rev. edn (Carmarthen: Independent Thinking Press, 2012), p. 29.

The T code should be written at the top of each students' assessment, depending on what they got wrong.

- At the start of the lesson, share with the students what each T code means and ask each of them to write out the target that corresponds to their T code.
- Having marked the assessments, produce a PowerPoint detailing the exam questions the students struggled with and how they relate to each T code.
- Talk the students through the questions, including why they lost marks and how to get full marks (perhaps include some exemplar answers to share with them). This stage is important: if you don't tell the students why they got it wrong in the first place, they will just get it wrong again if they are asked to repeat the task.
- The students should then be given another exam question that relates to their T code. This should not just be a repeat of the question they got wrong, but a different question (although still on the same topic).
- Share the mark scheme with the students who can then mark the new question themselves.

A note of caution here. We need to ensure that the feedback each student receives, and is then given work on, actually relates to what they don't understand. For example, a student could be given a question about lung structure and function and miss marks on it. As a result, they could then be given supportive input and further questions on lung structure. However, on further examination of their performance on the question, it could be the case that they have a good understanding of lung structure but don't really understand gaseous exchange and diffusion. With this in mind, the support and further questions they should be given would focus on this specific aspect.

6. Mark and annotate

This strategy is very much linked to DIRT. When marking a set of tests/assessments, always have a blank copy of the paper and the mark scheme to hand. Then, as you are marking it, you can note down the following on the paper and mark scheme:

- Common mistakes the students made, suggesting a lack of understanding or misconception.
- Questions where a number of students scored zero marks, suggesting that they really didn't get that topic.
- Specific words/phrases from the mark scheme that they didn't use and so lost marks. For example, they may have said, "Root hair cells have a high surface area to absorb water," whereas the mark scheme actually requires, "Root hair cells have a high surface area to increase the uptake of water by osmosis."

As you work through the paper with the students, you can be very specific about where and why they lost marks. It will also help you to identify which topics will need to be retaught and where the emphasis will need to be.

7. Mini whiteboards

The mini whiteboard, when used well, can be a useful tool for teachers because it can give you instant feedback about how well a class have understood a particular scientific idea.

In order to use them effectively, the following points are worth considering:

- They are best used to check objective-type questions that have a right or wrong answer (e.g. Which part of the cell contains chromosomes? If an object moves 30 metres in 15 seconds, what is its speed? What is the balanced chemical equation for photosynthesis?). Multiple-choice questions obviously lend themselves well to this. This makes it very easy to check the knowledge of the whole class.
- Ask the question, give the students thinking time and then count them down (3, 2, 1, show) so they all show their responses at the same time. This avoids them waiting for the 'clever student' to hold up their whiteboard, copying what they have written and then holding up the answer.
- Interrogate them on their answers (e.g. Why did you pick that answer? How did you come up with that answer? Where do you think you went wrong with that answer? Can you explain what that means?). Once the students know that you are going to do this, they will think more deeply about the responses they offer in future.
- If a number of students get the wrong answer, use this as feedback and reteach that particular topic.
- If you are using the whiteboards at the end of the lesson, use it as an opportunity to retrieve information from previous lessons by adding in questions from last lesson, last week and last month.

8. Verbal feedback

Verbal feedback is the bread and butter of the science teacher – it should never be underestimated, and nor should it require a verbal feedback stamp! These stamps have no real impact on student performance and are only really used as an accountability tool, and this is a questionable reason to ask teachers to do something. Verbal feedback should be just that: the teacher telling the student how to get better. From the point of view of the science teacher, this could focus on a number of aspects:

- To deepen their thinking around scientific ideas and encourage them to link scientific ideas together.
- To improve their written work, including responses to examination questions.
- To reflect upon and improve the presentation of their work.
- To make sure they are carrying out practical work safely and effectively.
- To fine tune specific practical methods they are using (e.g. accurately taking measurements).
- To encourage them to identify trends in results and offer explanations for these trends.
- To encourage them to evaluate experimental procedures they have used and consider possible improvements.

However, as has already been mentioned, once this feedback has been given there has to be an expectation that the student will do something about it. The 'repeat after me' strategy is useful here:

- Give the student verbal feedback – for example, "As well as describing the changes in the velocity of a falling object, you need to explain it using forces."
- Get the student to repeat the feedback back to you in their own words.
- Ask the student, "So what is the first thing you are going to do?" and wait for them to tell you.
- Return to the student in five minutes and check they have completed the improvement.

Positive self-verbalisation is another important form of verbal feedback. This involves getting the students to think about why they have been successful by asking them these questions:

- How did you get to that answer?
- Why did you do it like that?
- Did you use any unsuccessful methods before coming up with this successful one?
- What was difficult about it?
- What makes it a good answer?
- What advice would you give to anyone else who is struggling?

9. Highlighter action

This strategy can be used when students either spell a scientific word incorrectly or use a less scientific word where a more accurate word could be used (e.g. 'thick' instead of 'viscous'). While students are working, prowl the room with a highlighter pen. When you spot a piece of work in which the language could be developed further, highlight it and move away. Tell the class beforehand that if you do this, it means that they have to improve the vocabulary in that piece of work. The smart thing about this strategy is that it gets the students thinking about what the mistake is and how to address it. Come back in five minutes to see how they have got on.

Reflective Questions

- Does your feedback help you and the students know whether or not they are secure with the key knowledge?
- Does your feedback encourage the students to think about how they could improve their work?
- Do you ensure that the students respond to the feedback you give them?
- Is the feedback that you use manageable and sustainable?
- Do you use feedback to help you inform your planning?
- If you use peer or self-feedback, how do you ensure that it doesn't compound misconceptions?

A Final Thought (or Sixteen!)

While the six principles that have been discussed in this book are based around evidence from cognitive science and well-respected educational thinkers, they are also very much informed by the work of the brilliant science teachers I have been fortunate enough to work with over the years.

Without exception, they all have the highest expectations of the students they teach and then challenge all students, regardless of their starting point, to meet these expectations. They are very skilled at explaining complex scientific ideas in a clear and accessible manner, and then showing the students how to use this new knowledge. They then give the students the opportunity to practise using the new information and associated skills themselves, while supporting them to improve with carefully constructed questioning and feedback.

While an understanding of this pedagogy is important, it only works because of another vital attribute that all of these teachers have: the ability to build strong and productive relationships with the students they teach. Only when teachers are able to do this can they really implement these pedagogical principles effectively.

How do they do this?

1 They have the highest possible expectations of the students they teach. Students will either live up or down to your expectations of them, so expect excellence in everything they do – their work, their behaviour, their effort, the presentation of their work, their manners. Everything!

2 They praise students' effort – not intelligence or just doing the basics, but the effort and conscientiousness they put into their work.

3 They know the names of the students they teach. Take the time and effort to learn the names of your students. This demonstrates that you have a genuine interest in them as people and makes it much easier to direct questions at them or give them specific praise.

4 They make it their business to know their students as people too. Find out what the students can do, what they struggle with, what frustrates them and so on. Only then can you really know how and when to push them that bit more, when to step back and let them struggle or when to go in and offer some support to avoid them slipping into the panic zone.

5 They do smile before Christmas. You have to spend a lot of time together, so be nice! Young people are interesting and funny. Enjoy their company, and show them that you enjoy their company. Don't take yourself too seriously, but never forget the seriousness of your job.

6 They always act like the adult and accept that students are children. Model respectful language, dignity and how to be pleasant to others. Don't linger on an issue; deal with it and start afresh next lesson.

7 They build bridges. Find something to help you connect with your students, especially the students who can be more challenging. This could be as simple as finding out that they attend the local swimming club outside of school and taking an interest in how they are doing by asking them about it.

8 They engage students by showing a passion for science. Don't worry about engaging them with fun, gimmicky activities. Demonstrate a real passion for your subject and make this enthusiasm infectious! We should all want

our students to be as amazed at the wonders of science as we are, and enjoy our lessons for this reason.

9 They are eternal optimists – see number 8!

10 They believe in the students they teach. Make your students believe that they can achieve way beyond their expectations. You might be one of the only adults in their lives who does this.

11 They talk to all of their students about their work. Look at it, talk to them about what is so good about it and then push them to improve it and make it even better. If you expect them to work hard at it, you should value what they are doing. Don't just do this with the ones who crave your attention.

12 They find the small successes of their students and celebrate them. We can't just expect them to be motivated, we have to build their motivation by acknowledging their successes.

13 They are honest with their students. If their work or effort is poor, don't patronise them by telling them it's okay. Tell them the truth and then support them to improve it.

14 They never give up on them. Help your students to build grit and resilience by keeping them going, even when the going is really tough – and when they might be really tough on you! Show an unfaltering belief that they can get there.

15 They know their subject inside out. Not only will this mean that you teach it really well, but it will also make students confident about your ability to teach them really well. They want to feel secure and that they are in safe hands.

16 They say hello to their students (by name) in the corridor – because it's a friendly thing to do.

Finally, remind yourself of this on a daily basis, from the brilliant John Tomsett: "Ultimately, never forget that the best pastoral care for students from the most deprived socio-economic backgrounds is a great set of examination results."[1]

1 John Tomsett, This Much I Know About Professional Practice, in Rachel Jones (ed.), *Don't Change the Light Bulbs: A Compendium of Expertise from the UK's Most Switched-On Educators* (Carmarthen: Independent Thinking Press, 2014), p. 3.

Bibliography

Abrahams, Ian and Robin Millar (2008). Does Practical Work Really Work? A Study of the Effectiveness of Practical Work as a Teaching and Learning Method in School Science, *International Journal of Science Education* 30(14): 1945–1969.

Allison, Shaun (2014). Teaching with Pam, *Class Teaching* (6 April). Available at: https://classteaching.wordpress.com/2014/04/06/teaching-with-pam/.

Allison, Shaun and Andy Tharby (2015). *Making Every Lesson Count: Six Principles to Support Great Teaching and Learning* (Carmarthen: Crown House Publishing).

Beck, Isabel L., Margaret G. McKeown and Linda Kucan (2002). *Bringing Words to Life: Robust Vocabulary Instruction* (New York: Guilford Press).

Beere, Jackie (2012). *The Perfect (Ofsted) Lesson*, rev. edn (Carmarthen: Independent Thinking Press).

Brown, Peter C., Henry L. Roediger III and Mark A. McDaniel (2014). *Make It Stick: The Science of Successful Learning* (Cambridge, MA: Harvard University Press).

Coe, Robert, Cesare Aloisi, Steve Higgins and Lee Elliott Major (2014). *What Makes Great Teaching? Review of the Underpinning Research.* Project Report (London: Sutton Trust). Available at: http://www.suttontrust.com/wp-content/uploads/2014/10/What-makes-great-teaching-FINAL-4.11.14.pdf.

Department for Education (2011). *The National Strategies 1997–2011.* Available at: https://www.gov.uk/government/publications/the-national-strategies-1997-to-2011.

Didau, David (2016). A Definition of Learning, *The Learning Spy* (28 January). Available at: http://www.learningspy.co.uk/learning/a-definition-of-learning/.

Dunlosky, John, Katherine A. Rawson, Elizabeth J. Marsh, Mitchell J. Nathan and Daniel T. Willingham (2013). Improving Students' Learning with Effective Learning Techniques: Promising Directions from Cognitive and Educational Psychology, *Psychological Science in the Public Interest* 14(1): 4–58.

Dweck, Carol (2006). *Mindset: Changing the Way You Think to Fulfil Your Potential* (London: Robinson).

Harlen, Wynne (ed.) (2015). *Working with Big Ideas in Science Education* (Trieste: Science Education Programme). Available at: http://www.ase.org.uk/documents/working-with-the-big-ideas-in-science-education/.

Hattie, John (2014). The Science of Learning. Keynote speech presented at Osiris World-Class Schools Convention, London.

Independent Teacher Workload Review Group (2016). *Eliminating Unnecessary Workload Around Marking* (London: Department for Education). Available at: https://www.gov.uk/government/uploads/system/uploads/attachment_data/file/511256/Eliminating-unnecessary-workload-around-marking.pdf.

Kahneman, Daniel (2011). *Thinking, Fast and Slow* [Kindle edn] (London: Allen Lane).

Keogh, Brenda and Stuart Naylor (2000). *Concept Cartoons in Science Education* (Sandbach: Millgate House Publishers).

Kirby, Joe (2015). Knowledge Organisers, *Pragmatic Education* (28 March). Available at: https://pragmaticreform.wordpress.com/2015/03/28/knowledge-organisers/.

Lemov, Doug (2010). *Teach Like a Champion: 49 Techniques that Put Students on the Path to College* [Kindle edn] (San Francisco, CA: Jossey-Bass).

Miller, George A. (1956). The Magical Number Seven, Plus or Minus Two: Some Limits on Our Capacity for Processing Information, *Psychological Review* 63(2): 81–97.

Moyse, Chris (2016). Talk Like … Resources (28 March). Available at: https://chrismoyse.wordpress.com/2016/03/28/talk-like-resources/.

Quigley, Alex (2016). *The Confident Teacher: Developing Successful Habits of Mind, Body and Pedagogy* (Abingdon: Routledge).

Sweller, John (1994). Cognitive Load Theory, Learning Difficulty, and Instructional Design, *Learning and Instruction* 4: 295–312. Available at: http://www.realtechsupport.org/UB/I2C/Sweller_CognitiveLoadTheory_1994.pdf.

Tharby, Andy (2014). Probing the Continuum, *Reflecting English* (16 January). Available at: https://reflectingenglish.wordpress.com/2014/01/16/simply-the-best-post-it-note-discussion-rocks/.

Tomsett, John (2014). This Much I Know About Professional Practice, in Rachel Jones (ed.), *Don't Change the Light Bulbs: A Compendium of Expertise from the UK's Most Switched-On Educators* (Carmarthen: Independent Thinking Press).

Wiliam, Dylan (2014). Is the Feedback You're Giving Students Helping or Hindering? *Dylan Wiliam Center* (29 November). Available at: http://www.dylanwiliamcenter.com/is-the-feedback-you-are-giving-students-helping-or-hindering/.

Wiliam, Dylan and Paul Black (1990). *Inside the Black Box: Raising Standards Through Classroom Assessment* (London: GL Assessment).

Willingham, Daniel T. (2008–2009). What Will Improve a Student's Memory? *American Educator* (winter): 17–25. Available at: http://www.aft.org/sites/default/files/periodicals/willingham_0.pdf.

Willingham, Daniel T. (2010). *Why Don't Students Like School? A Cognitive Scientist Answers Questions About How the Mind Works and What It Means for the Classroom* (San Francisco, CA: Jossey-Bass).

Making Every Maths Lesson Count

Six principles to support great teaching and learning

Kate Blight

ISBN: 978-178583180-5

Writing in an engaging style, full-time teacher Kate Blight offers practical strategies to support the maths teacher in the secondary school. The book offers gimmick-free ideas which support the six tried-and-tested principles from the award-winning *Making Every Lesson Count.*

The book is held together by six pedagogical principles – challenge, explanation, modelling, practice, feedback and questioning – and provides simple, realistic strategies that maths teachers can use to develop the teaching and learning in their classrooms.

The book will support established teachers and those new to the profession to enable their students to make progress.

For maths teachers of pupils aged 11–16.

Making Every Primary Lesson Count

Six principles to support great teaching and learning

Jo Payne and Mel Scott

ISBN: 978-178583181-2

In *Making Every Primary Lesson Count*, full-time primary teachers Jo Payne and Mel Scott share easy, effective strategies for ensuring that every lesson makes a difference for young learners. Written in the engaging style of the award-winning *Making Every Lesson Count*, the book shares practical advice grounded in educational research and is suitable for teachers of the Early Years and Key Stages 1 and 2.

The book is held together by six pedagogical principles – challenge, explanation, modelling, practice, feedback and questioning – and provides simple, realistic classroom strategies that all primary teachers can embed immediately.

At the heart of the strategies are excellence and growth: ensuring teachers and pupils can aim high and put in the effort required to be successful. Tried-and-tested, gimmick-free teaching strategies from across the curriculum and all primary year groups are shared.

The ideas will have a high impact on learning in the classroom without diminishing teachers' work–life balance. The strategies enable pupils to leave primary school as confident, successful learners, equipped with the skills and knowledge required of them.

Suitable for all Early Years and primary teachers.

Making Every English Lesson Count

Six principles to support great reading and writing

Andy Tharby

ISBN: 978-178583179-9

Writing in the practical, engaging style of the award-winning *Making Every Lesson Count*, Andy Tharby returns with an offering of gimmick-free advice that combines the time-honoured wisdom of excellent English teachers with the most useful evidence from cognitive science.

Making Every English Lesson Count is underpinned by six pedagogical principles – challenge, explanation, modelling, practice, feedback and questioning – and provides simple, realistic classroom strategies to bring the teaching of conceptual knowledge, vocabulary and challenging literature to the foreground.

In an age of educational quick fixes, GCSE reform and ever-moving goalposts, this precise and timely book provides practical solutions to perennial problems and inspires a rich, challenging and evidence-informed approach to English teaching.

Suitable for English teachers of students aged 11–16 years.

Making Every Lesson Count

Six principles to support great teaching and learning

Shaun Allison and Andy Tharby

ISBN: 978-184590973-4

Packed with practical strategies and case studies, *Making Every Lesson Count* bridges the gap between research findings and classroom practice. The authors examine the evidence behind what makes great teaching, and how to implement this in the classroom to make a difference to learning. Using case studies from a number of schools, the authors demonstrate how an ethos of excellence and growth can be built through high-quality classroom practice. Combining robust evidence from a range of fields with the practical wisdom of experienced, effective classroom teachers, the book is a must-read for trainee teachers, experienced teachers wishing to enhance their practice and school leaders looking for an evidence-based alternative to restrictive Ofsted-driven definitions of great teaching.

A toolkit of strategies that teachers can use every lesson to make that lesson count. No gimmicky teaching – just high-impact and focused teaching that results in great learning, every lesson, every day.

ERA Educational Book Award winner 2016. Judges' comments: "A highly practical and interesting resource with loads of information and uses to support and inspire teachers of all levels of experience. An essential staffroom book."